SURVIVAL SWIMMING

SWIMMING TRAINING FOR ESCAPE AND SURVIVAL

SAM FURY

Illustrated by
YOPI MUHAMAD

CONTENTS

Introduction	1
General Water Safety	3

EFFICIENT SWIMMING

Treading Water	7
Swimming Fast	12
Swimming Long Distance	37
Swimming Long Distance Underwater	48

WATER SAFETY, SELF-RESCUE, AND SURVIVAL

Protective Clothing	61
Safe Entry Techniques	65
Survival Swimming Styles	71
Waves	73
Tides and Currents	77
Obstructions	80
River Crossings	91
Self-Rescue Bowline	115
Inflating Your Clothes	117
Cold Water Survival	121
Flood	127
Survival at Sea	129
Bonus Freebies	138
Author Recommendations	139
Survival Fitness Plan Training Manuals	141
About the Author	145

Copyright Sam Fury © 2018

www.SurvivalFitnessPlan.com/Sam-Fury-Amazon

All Rights Reserved
No part of this document may be reproduced without written consent from the author.

This publication has the approval of Bert Luxing, creator of the Survival Fitness Plan.

WARNINGS AND DISCLAIMERS

The information in this publication is made public for reference only.

Neither the author, publisher, nor anyone else involved in the production of this publication is responsible for how the reader uses the information or the result of his/her actions.

Consult a physician before undertaking any new form of physical activity.

INTRODUCTION

Swimming is a very important skill when it comes to survival. There are too many stories of people that have drowned needlessly because they didn't know how to swim efficiently in specific situations.

Swimming is also fun and beneficial to the body. It is a low impact form of exercise with great cardiovascular advantages.

This book was first published in 2014. It was an instructional manual on how to learn the best swimming strokes for survival. It is updated in 2018 by combining the original contents with part 1 and sections of part 2 of the Swim Workouts and Water Rescue manual.

This book is split into 2 parts.

Efficient Swimming

This section has techniques and training methods for improving your ability in swimming:

- Fast
- Long distance
- Underwater (speed and distance)

Water Safety, Self-Rescue, and Survival

Being near any body of water has its inherent dangers, and open water has even more. This section has information on the different dangers in various forms of open water. It explains what to do when faced with these dangers, covering self-rescue and survival in solo and group scenarios.

In this manual, the term "open water" refers to any natural body of water such as oceans, lakes, and rivers.

GENERAL WATER SAFETY

The activities in this manual can be dangerous if you do not take the proper precautions. Follow the water safety guidelines in this and other sections.

Important! Whenever possible, learn new techniques in calm waters (such as a pool). Only when you are confident should you practice them in open water.

- The best way to ensure safety is to avoid the danger in the first place. If total avoidance is not an option, the next best thing is to seek out local knowledge. Ask lifeguards, local surfers, paddlers, fisherman, etc. Also, scout it out yourself as circumstances may change.
- Always have a safety person present, e.g., a training partner or lifeguard.
- Protect yourself from the sun with appropriate clothing and sunscreen.
- Stay hydrated.
- Keep warm. This is covered in detail in Part 2 of this manual.
- Don't go near water under the influence of drugs or alcohol.
- It is good to push yourself for improvement, but be careful not to push yourself too much. This is especially true in open water.
- Have the correct safety and rescue equipment nearby, and know how to use it.
- Train only in waters and conditions you know to be safe. Look for signs and flags for the information you

need, and if you are unsure, ask the lifeguards. Don't swim when the red flag is flying.
- Watch out for other people doing recreational activities, such as surfing or motorsports. Usually, they will have separate designated areas from swimmers.
- Never run or dive into the unknown water. In open water, you must always check as conditions can change.
- If you get into trouble, stay calm and raise your arm to signal for help.
- Always wear a life vest when in a boat or any uncontrolled environment. Zip it up! A loose vest can get caught on many things.
- Tell someone that is not going with you where you will be training and when you expect to be back.
- Take care near any water edge whether it be a pool, riverbank, etc.
- Learn about the different characteristics of various water bodies before training in them.
- Enter and exit the water in a safe manner using the designated entry and exit points, e.g., the ladder. Use your hands and feet, and take your time.

EFFICIENT SWIMMING

This section has techniques and training methods for improving your ability in swimming:

- Fast
- Long distance
- Underwater (speed and distance)

TREADING WATER

Treading water is the most energy-efficient way to stay in one spot.

Learn to tread water before doing any other water-based training. This is so if you need to you can tread water until you either create a plan for self-rescue or help arrives.

When first learning to tread water, do so in shallow water and with a lifeguard present. Progress to deep water when confident.

While treading water your body is vertical in the water and your head is above the surface. Your arms and legs work to keep you afloat. Torso movement is minimal.

There are a few ways to tread water. The following method is a little harder to get the hang of but it is the most energy efficient. It combines vertical sculling with your arms and the eggbeater kick.

Sculling

To skull, move your arms horizontal in the water, back and forth — not up and down.

Turn your palms in the direction that your arms are moving. Angle your thumbs a little up on the way in, and your pinky fingers a little up on the way out.

Keep your back straight. Don't lean forward or backward.

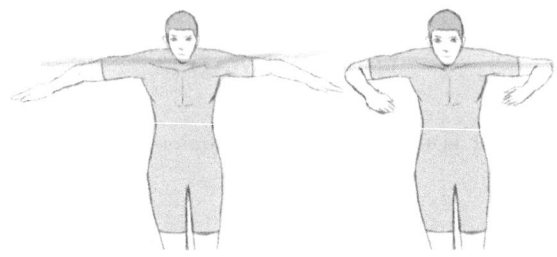

Vary the width of your stroke. Sometimes your hands remain far apart, and sometimes they almost come together.

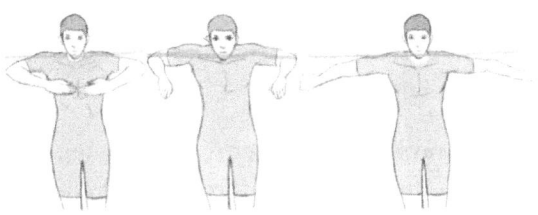

You can start by practicing this in shallow water. Find a depth where you can keep your head above water whilst you kneel down.

Begin the sculling action with your hands, enough to raise your knees off the bottom.

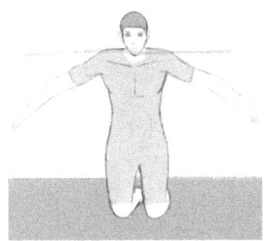

When you are ready, move into deeper water. Have your feet directly underneath you, toes pointing straight down.

Eggbeater Kick (Rotary Kick)

The egg-beater kick can be tricky to learn but it is worth going through the trouble. In comparison to the alternatives (such as the flutter kick), it is the most energy efficient.

Move your legs like an eggbeater, each leg rotating a different direction. It is like a breast-stroke kick done one leg at a time. When one leg kicks out, the other should be coming in.

To begin learning the egg-beater kick do it on dry land by sitting on the edge of a chair. Sit up straight and move only your right leg in a counter-clockwise circle.

Next, move only your left leg in a clockwise circle.

When you are ready, join these two leg movements together. As your right leg goes out, your left leg comes in. At all times one leg comes in while the other goes out.

Once you have the coordination, practice the egg-beater kick in the water.

Lift your toes as you press down, so that your flat foot pushes down on the water, helping to propel you up.

Also, point your toes as you bring your foot up so that you have less resistance.

Do not extend your legs completely. If they become straight you will lose upwards propulsion.

Treading Water

Once proficient at sculling and the eggbeater kick you can stay afloat by doing ONLY one or the other.

You can perform tasks with your hands while staying afloat in one spot, and/or you can stay afloat in case of a leg injury.

By putting the two actions together you conserve energy in both your arms and legs. This is ideal in a survival situation when you need to stay in one spot for long periods of time.

When treading water, stay calm and slow down your breathing rhythm. This will maximize your conservation of energy.

SWIMMING FAST

You will need to swim fast in emergency situations such as rescue or escape. Race swimming techniques are a base. They are then adapted for use in emergency situations.

There are three basic elements to consider when your goal is swimming fast.

1. Entry and/or Initial propulsion
2. Underwater swim
3. Surface swimming

Your initial propulsion is usually either a dive entry or by pushing off something.

Once you have your initial propulsion you want to swim as fast and for as long as you can underwater. Use the fly-kick (either dolphin or fish tale).

Swimming underwater is faster than surface swimming due to less resistance. When speed is your goal, swim underwater for as long as possible.

Finally, once you need to surface for air, use freestyle (a.k.a. over-arm, front-crawl) since it is the fastest surface-swimming stroke.

It is assumed that you already know the basics of the above three elements. Now we concentrate on improvement in the two factors needed to maximize speed for each element, i.e.,

- Decreasing drag
- Improving propulsion

Entry and Initial Propulsion

There are different entry and/or initial propulsion techniques which you can use. The one you choose depends on the situation.

- Push-off
- Shallow dive
- Dolphin dive
- Deep-water floating start
- Flip Turn and push-off

When speed is your primary goal, all these actions will lead into the underwater fly-kick.

Note: When you need to enter unknown waters, use the safe entry techniques described in Part 2 of this manual. Opting for a safer entry technique may slow you down, but you won't be very fast at swimming if you get injured. Safety first, always.

Push-off / Streamlined Position

For the greatest speed when pushing-off the edge, drop below the water 1 to 3 feet. When doing a flip turn this will be automatic.

The best position for your legs/feet is shoulder width apart and with a bend in your knees. Push hard off the edge with strong legs and a tight core.

When you push off your body must be as streamlined as possible. Become a straight arrow, stretching your body from your toes to your fingertips.

Place the palm of one hand on the back of the other. Wrap your upper hand's pinky and thumb around your lower hand and then raise them over your head. Point your fingers in the direction you are going.

Straighten your arms. Tuck them behind your head and squeeze your shoulder blades together. Another method is to squeeze your ears between your biceps.

Keep your head down (swimming down-hill) with the top of your head pointing in the direction you want to go.

Point your feet and turn your toes in towards each other a little (pigeon-toed).

Keep your chin tucked and use a smooth exhale in whatever way is most comfortable for you.

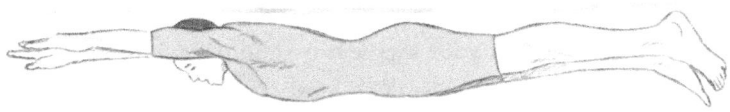

Maintain this streamline position as you push off the wall. Start the underwater fly-kick to maintain momentum underwater before surfacing into freestyle.

Note: Being on your side (as opposed to facing down) creates less resistance and you may gain some speed. You should experiment with this.

Diving

Diving will give you the most propulsion but is also the most dangerous entry method.

Important! If you are unsure of the water depth and/or what lies below the surface, DO NOT DIVE!

In an emergency situation, you may be pretty sure it is safe to dive but do not have the time for a thorough assessment.

For this reason, use the shallow dive.

A shallow dive is when you "arc" into the water hands first whilst you adopt the streamlined position.

When starting to perfect your dive, do so from a stationary position.

Place your lead (strongest) leg on the edge of the water (e.g. poolside) with your toes a little over the edge. Your rear foot is flat on the ground.

Balance your weight evenly on both feet. Place your arms above your head in the streamlined position, with your chin tucked to your chest.

Push off with your lead foot so you get some distance.

Arc over as you push.

Adopt the streamline position as you enter the water.

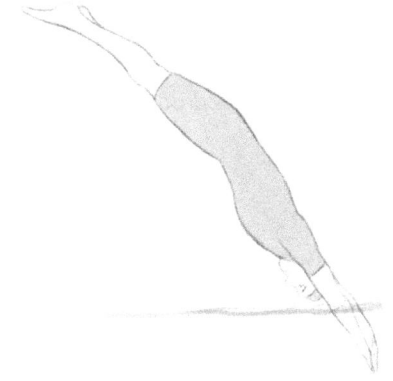

Once you are in the water, hold your head up and arch your back. This will steer your body up away from the bottom.

The more you arch, the more speed you will lose. You have to compromise depending on the water depth. Also remember, that you will be faster streamlining a couple of feet below the surface.

Note: *Do not look/arch up before you are in the water. You will lose speed and may get injured.*

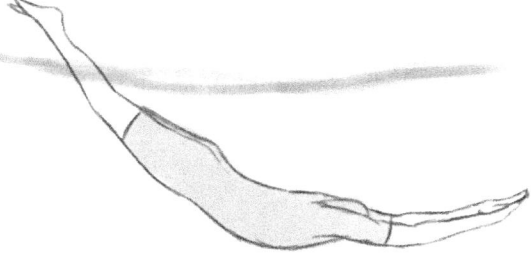

When you're ready, try diving from a walking and then a running start. In this case, your arms will start by your sides. Once you leap off the edge adopt the correct position so you can enter the water using the same basic form.

Dolphin Dive

Dolphin dives are useful when running into the water in a beach scenario. It will allow you to overcome waist/chest deep water as fast as possible. Run until the water is knee/waist high and then use the dolphin dive.

As you run in, be vigilant for obstacles in the terrain, e.g., rocks or holes. Once you hit the water, lift your feet completely out of the water for as long as possible. This decreases "drag time".

Put your hands in the streamline position and leap/arc over into a dive. Do this before the water decreases your forward momentum. Roughly knee to waist deep.

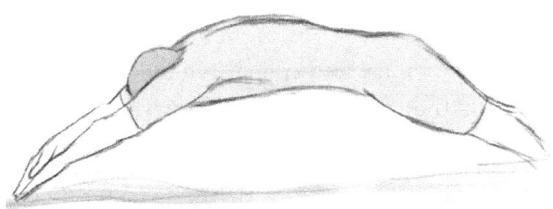

Don't dive too hard (you might injure yourself) but dive deep enough to grab the sand on the bottom. Grab hold of the sand and lock your feet in one in front of the other. Push forward off the ground as fast as you can into your next dolphin dive. Continue to dolphin dive in rapid succession until it is too deep to continue (about neck deep).

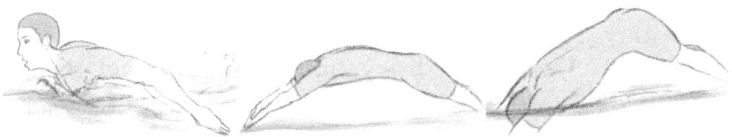

Do not look up whilst dolphin diving. Like in the shallow dive, this is important for safety and speed.

If a wave is approaching, dolphin dive under it, grab the sand and stay under until the wave passes over you.

Once it is too deep to dolphin dive, transition into the underwater fly-kick.

You can use the dolphin dive to come back into shore also. Swim until it is shallow enough to dolphin dive, then continue to dolphin dive until you can run out.

Floating Start

Use a floating start from a floating/treading position when you have nothing to push off.

The key for this is to use an explosive initial kick (such as a side scissor kick) and then go straight into freestyle.

If you know that you will need a floating start, get as close to the freestyle position as possible.

Adopt a horizontal position. Place your dominant hand in front, ready to pull back into your first stroke. Have your other arm in a half-stroke position. Your heels should be close to the surface of the water. Tread water in this position.

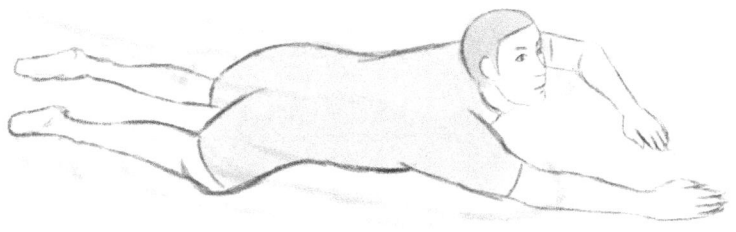

When it is time to swim kick hard as you pull with your first stroke and transition into normal freestyle.

Flip Turns

Flip turns are often identified with swimming races in a pool. In an emergency situation having to turn in the water is not likely, but it is possible. Knowing how to flip turn will make it much faster.

First, learn the flip turn without having to push off the wall. In an emergency situation, this is most likely the style you will use, and it also makes it easier to learn.

The main flip part of the flip turn is actually only a half-flip. Start by swimming on your stomach (e.g., freestyle). As your arm enters the water for the turn, start a half-flip by tucking your chin and doing a small dolphin kick. At the same time, move your hands to your sides. Breath out through your nose to prevent any water getting up it.

Continue the half-flip by tucking your knees towards your eyes and your feet to your bum. At the same time, push down with the palms of your hands to get your feet over your head. Keep your elbows close to your body while doing this.

As you complete the half-flip, bring your arms into the streamline position. You are now pointing in your new direction of travel.

Roll onto your stomach by twisting your hands a little and looking in the direction you want to rotate. Don't turn your head, only move your eyes.

Use an explosive kick and arm pull to set you off in your new direction like you would in a floating start.

Note: Don't try to look where you are going during the flip. It will slow you down and mess up your co-ordination. Look at your knees instead.

To turn and push off a wall (such as in a pool swimming race) speed up (kick harder) when you are about 5 meters away from the wall. Ensure you have enough air to make the turn, but don't take a breath before it as you will slow down.

Once you are a bit more than an arm's length away from the wall, do the turn as normal. Push off the wall as described before (Push-off / Streamlined Position). The difference is that you will be face up when you do the push off, toes pointing up.

Once you push off, start to turn onto your stomach and then do underwater fly-kicks.

You may wish to start to fly-kick before (whilst on your back) and/or during your turn also. Experiment to discover what you prefer/works best for you.

Continue to fly-kick until you need to start surface swimming.

Once you can do the basic turn and push off, work on perfecting your distance in relation to the wall. Land your feet with your knees bent close to 90° and your hips bent close to 110°.

Underwater Fly Kick

When you know how to do it, swimming underwater is faster than swimming on the surface of it. When you want to go fast, swim underwater for as long as you can.

The fastest way to swim underwater is using the underwater fly-kick.

There are two main ways to do the underwater fly-kick. The dolphin kick and the fish kick.

If you are good at it, the fish kick is faster than the dolphin kick, but in the SFP we focus on the dolphin kick because it is:

- Easier to master.
- Easier to control, especially in open water.
- Used in other strokes outlined in this manual.

Once you have the standard dolphin kick mastered, you may wish to progress to the fish-tale kick.

After your initial propulsion (e.g., dive or push-off) maintain your streamline position. You want to maximize this glide phase before you start kicking.

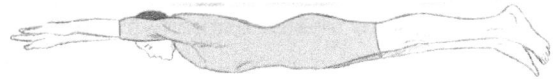

Just before you start to slow down, use both feet/legs at the same time to kick up and down. Keep your upper body in the streamline position.

Bend your knees so that your kicks finish/start well in front (or behind) your body, but do not kick from your knees. Use your core/hips to generate the power. To do this, suck in your tummy and squeeze your buttocks together.

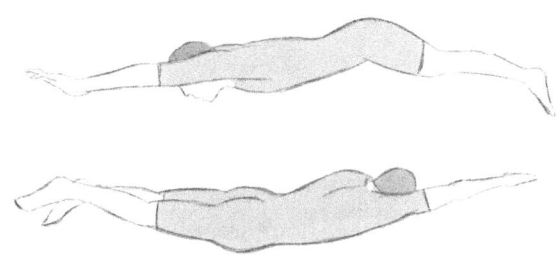

You must also snap your toes and ankle. It may help to think of your body as a whip. The power comes from your core (the handle), and your feet/toes are the tip of the whip which snap up and down. Kick fast and kick small.

Ensure you also kick backward instead of only up and down. You want to push the water behind you.

Your up and down kicks should be of equal force. Use the vertical kicking drill to develop your coordination and strength for this. The vertical kicking drill is in the freestyle chapter.

When you start to surface, begin freestyle.

Ankle Strength and Flexibility

Increasing your ankle strength and flexibility will improve your dolphin (and flutter) kick. Here are some exercises you can do.

Ankle rotations. Move your foot and ankle in a circle as large as possible without pain. Do 15-20 circles in each direction.

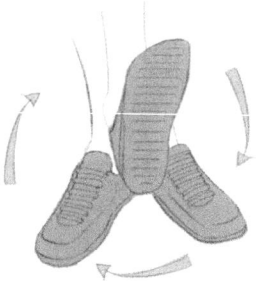

Ankle stretches. There are four levels of this exercise. Each increases in difficulty from the previous one.

From a standing position, place the top of your toes on the ground a half step behind your other foot. Push down and forward into the ground.

Sit on your heels, with your shins and the top of your feet flat on the ground.

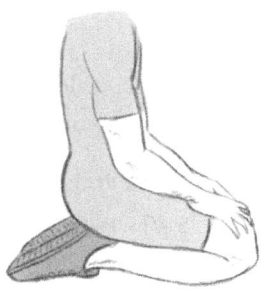

Lean back onto your hands to increase the stretch.

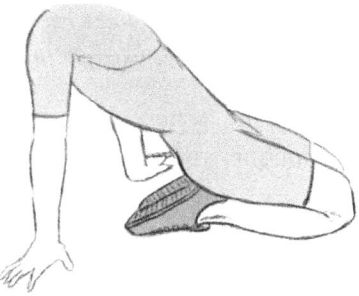

Finally, put your hands up in the streamline position and then lift your knees off the ground.

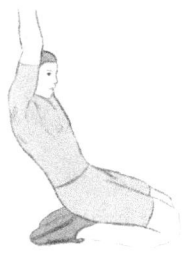

Ankle Inversion. From a standing position, roll one foot to the outside. Press the edge of your foot into the ground in a gentle manner. Only do one foot at a time.

Freestyle

This chapter assumes you already know the basic mechanics of swimming freestyle. If you don't, please see part 3 of this manual.

Freestyle (overarm) is the fastest way to surface swim. By improving your technique, you will become faster and more energy efficient.

There are a few different areas which you can "tweak". Practice in each individual area, and then put them all together when you are ready.

Balance

Being balanced in the water will make you more streamlined and so will increase your speed.

Maintain a position that is as horizontal as possible.

Except when taking a breath, keep your head down and your neck relaxed. Imagine you have a blowhole in the back of your neck that you have to keep open. Looking down (as opposed to forwards) will also help.

Breathing

Breathing while swimming (as opposed to holding your breath under-water) increases your stamina. Start blowing out as soon as you finish inhaling and continue to do so until you take your next breath.

Experiment with breathing rhythms (e.g. take a breath every 3rd or 5th stroke) to see what works best for you. It may help to count your arm strokes (e.g., 1, 2, 3, 4, breathe) or whatever method you prefer.

It is important to completely exhale before taking your next breath so that you get rid of all the stale air. This increases your stamina and keeps you streamlined for longer. Every time you breathe you are breaking your streamlined position.

Keep as close as possible to your streamlined position while breathing. Do this by turning your head as opposed to lifting it out of the water. Your mouth only needs to be a little bit out of the water to inhale. Your eye line should be no higher than to the side. If you're looking to the sky, you are turning your head way too much.

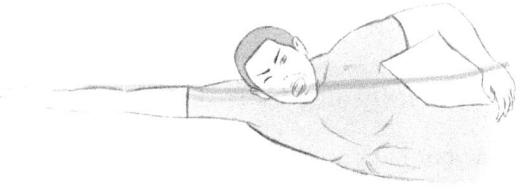

Breathing on alternate sides of your body (bilaterally) is a good habit.

Always inhale through your mouth, but try to exhale most of the air through your nose.

This is especially true when turning/flipping to avoid getting water up your nose.

Rolling

Roll from side to side with each arm stroke. This will engage your back muscles and improve propulsion.

Engage your core as you do it.

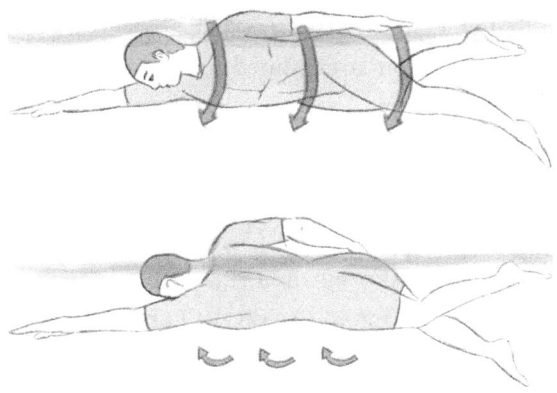

Rolling Drills

This drill is good for getting used to floating on your sides.

Float flat on your back and do a light flutter kick for propulsion. Keep your body straight with your arms at your sides. Apply downward pressure on the back of your head and on your shoulder blades so that your hips and legs buoy up.

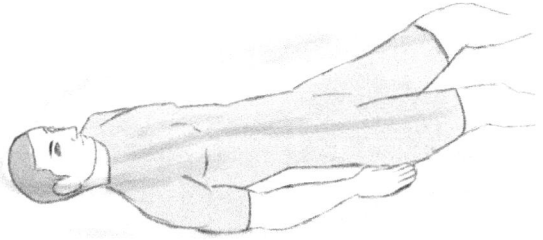

Once you feel balanced in this position, do the following:

- Roll onto your side so that your top arm and some of your top thigh clear the water.
- Your head does not move while you roll on your side. Keep looking at the sky and roll your body as one.
- Continue to flutter kick.

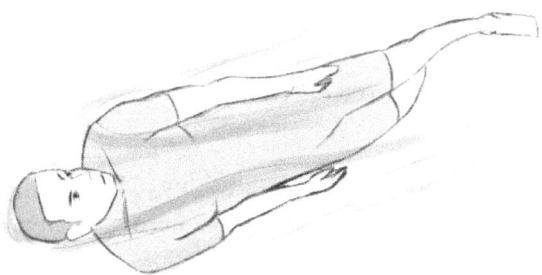

Roll as far as you are comfortable. A 45° body roll is good for most people.

Practice this on both sides of your body.

Once you are comfortable with the above, advance by rolling to 90° so you face down.

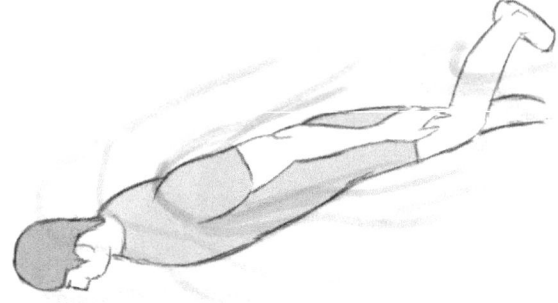

Keep flutter kicking and keep balanced. Continue to roll in the same direction until you are in the 45° body position, but on your opposite side.

Remember to roll your whole body together. Don't lead with your head.

When balanced, roll back the other way.

Arm Technique

The freestyle stroke is explained in four parts. The catch, pull, exit, and recovery. These four stages occur and repeat in the order listed.

There is a more advanced arm stroke known as the Early Vertical Forearm Position (EVF). It is harder to master, holds a greater risk of injury, and the gain in speed is minimal. It is more for elite competitive swimmers.

The following technique is like a non-extreme EVF.

Catch

The catch is when your hand first enters the water.

Create a "web" with your hand by spacing your fingers apart a little, about 30% of the diameter of one finger. Keep this spacing for the whole time.

As you roll your body, lengthen your arm out with your palm faced down. Angle your fingertips a little downward and flex your wrist. Point your middle finger in your direction of travel.

Enter your hand into the water fingertips first. Ensure your arm/hand does not cross your centerline.

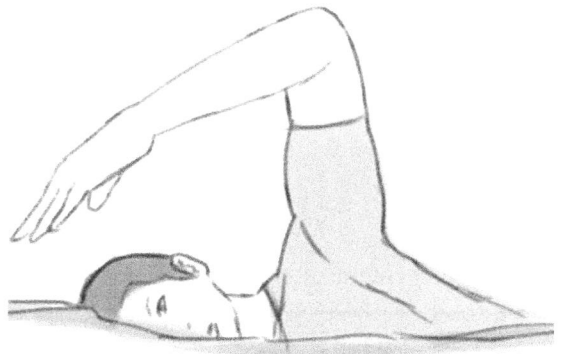

Once your hand is in the water, bend your elbow and press back on the water. Your forearm is in a near-vertical position.

Do not push forward once your hand is in the water. It is better to go straight into the pull phase of the stroke.

It may help to imagine your arm is moving over a big ball.

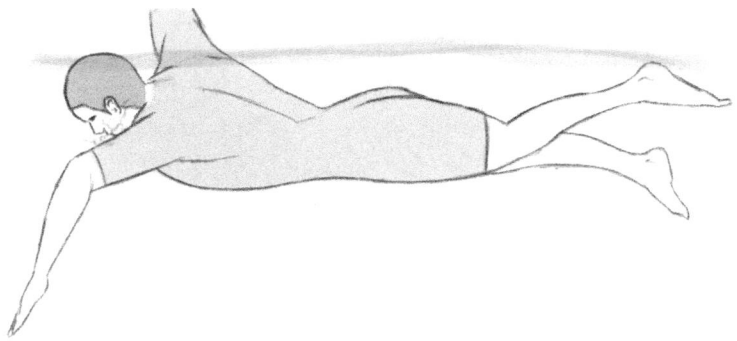

You can use finger paddles to help you perfect your catch. Wear them loose.

If you over-reach or have some other bad technique, the finger paddle will come off.

Another thing you can do is use a kick-board. Focus on a good catch with only one arm. The kick-board will prevent you reaching forward.

Pull

The pull is the movement of your arm in the water down the length of your body.

After doing a good catch your elbow will be in the "high" position. Your elbow faces the sky and your palm faces to your rear.

Keep this high elbow as you push the water behind you.

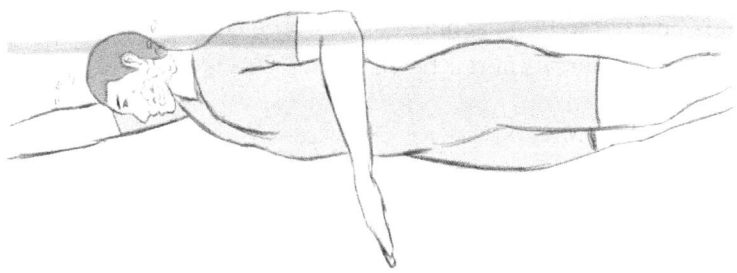

A good catch and pull is an easy, flowing feeling. You get great forward propulsion utilizing your pecks and lats.

Exit

This phase of your stroke is when your arm/hand leaves the water, just past your hip.

It is important not to be too eager to bring your arm out of the water. Push beyond your hip as if you are trying to reach your knee, using the same press-up motion you would when exiting a pool on the wall.

Do this push for the whole range of your pull, and as your thumb touches your thigh, flick the water out.

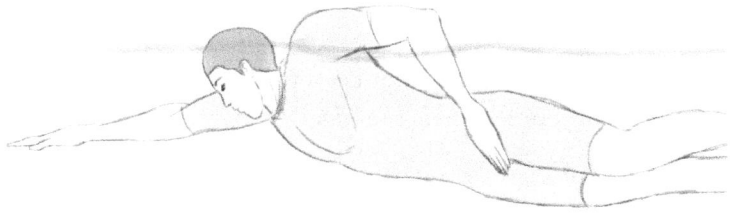

Recovery

The recovery is the time when your arm is in the air. It flicks out of the exit and then re-enters into the catch.

It is best not to think about your recovery. Let it take its natural path. Your mental effort is better spent focusing on a great catch.

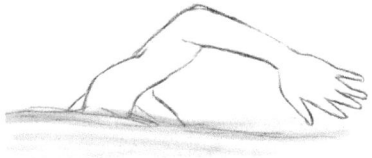

You can use stretch cords to practice all phases of your stroke on dry land. It is also useful for focusing on problem areas.

Efficient Kicking

A good kick is a compact one. It shouldn't be too low nor break the water's surface. Do not disturb your natural body alignment.

Move your feet/legs independently of each other. Push one down as you pull the other up. Putting energy into both the up and down strokes is important.

Use short, quick kicks with your whole leg, starting at the hip. Keep your legs long and straight, but not rigid. Have a slight, natural bend in your knees.

Point your toes behind you but keep your ankles relaxed. Only the bottom of your feet meet the water's surface.

Find a rhythm that is comfortable and stick with it. Around 15 kicks every 10 seconds is good.

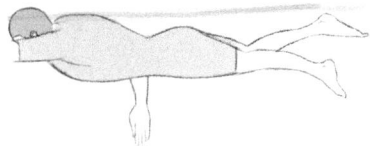

Vertical Kicking Drill

This vertical kicking drill will help to improve your flutter kick. It is also good for your dolphin kick.

Do this drill in deep water, but make sure you are near something you can hold onto when you get tired.

Be vertical in the water and do nothing but flutter kicking to keep your mouth and nose above the surface. You will be kicking hard. Concentrate on correct kicking technique as described before.

Begin with your arms underwater and use a small sculling motion.

As you improve, try keeping your arms and hands tight against your body.

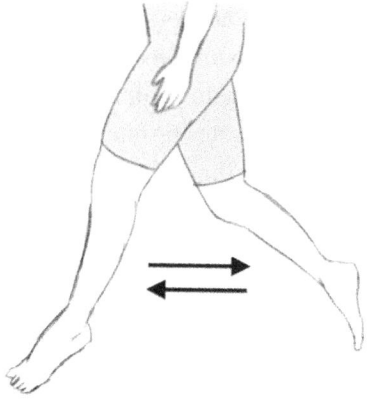

Advance further by raising your fingertips out of the water. Raise your arms higher and higher as you gain strength.

Transitioning from the Fly Kick to Freestyle

As you begin to surface begin to flutter kick and start to pull one of your arms down from the streamline position. Time the completion of your pull phase so that you arm exits the water as if you were doing freestyle all along. This takes practice.

Complete a few strokes before taking a breath and then continue into freestyle as normal.

Additional Tips for Improvement

You can adapt most of these tips to all areas of swimming, and life in general.

- **Train regularly,** at least twice a week.
- **Compete against your times.** Notice what causes you to swim faster and use what works best for you.
- **Identify and work on your weak points.**
- **Visualize someone chasing you.** Feel as if you are being chased, then work on calming your mind and body and concentrate on swimming as fast as you can.
- **Get a professional swim coach.** For those of you that are having difficulties or want to get to the next level.

SWIMMING LONG DISTANCE

There are two strokes to learn for swimming long-distance. Survival backstroke, and the combat side stroke.

Survival backstroke, a.k.a. elementary backstroke is an easy stroke to learn and is very energy efficient. It is for long distance and/or survival situations, e.g., waiting for rescue.

The combat side stroke (CSS) is an ultra-efficient variation of the sidestroke. It was developed by the navy seals and is perfect for escape, evasion, and survival.

- It is efficient (fast yet energy conserving)
- You can do it with gear (like a backpack)
- Your body profile is less (you'll be harder to see)
- It is excellent for swimming through the surf in open water
- You can observe your surroundings as you swim (unlike the survival backstroke)

Survival Backstroke

This chapter assumes you know the basic mechanics of survival backstroke. If you need to learn it from scratch, please see part 3 of this manual.

Survival backstroke is floating on your back as you propel through the water. You use a simultaneous frog/breaststroke kick and a sculling motion with your hands. Your arms and legs move and come together at the same time.

The main goal of the survival backstroke is to conserve energy and reduce heat loss.

To maximize energy conservation, do the survival backstroke very slow. Take short strokes and glide for as long as possible. Only take the next stroke when you feel your legs dropping or you loose forward momentum.

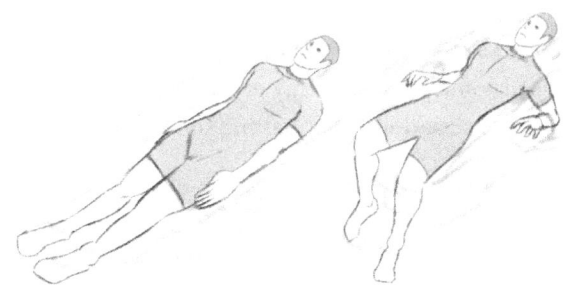

Taking short strokes minimizes heat loss from under your armpits and between your legs. Your arms should not extend beyond your shoulders.

Also, at the end of each stroke, bring your arms and legs together.

Hold them close but comfortable against your body.

Also use the survival backstroke is if an underwater explosion is likely. You will want to go faster so you can escape the blast, so make your strokes larger. Take your next stroke sooner than normal, but not too soon.

Make the most out of your streamlined glide position while achieving the most speed.

Combat Side Stroke

Combat Side Stroke (CSS) is a mix of freestyle, breaststroke, and sidestroke.

There are 4 basic stages to the CSS. The streamline position, two catch and pull movements, and the recovery. The recovery involves a scissor kick paired with a breaststroke-like arm movement.

Note: A lot of the terminology used in this chapter is explained in the freestyle section.

Streamline Position

Get some initial propulsion. Adopt the streamline position as explained in the Entry and Initial Propulsion chapter.

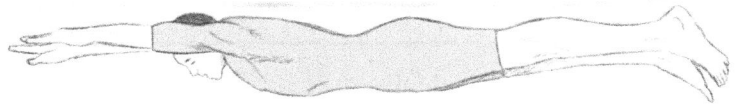

First Catch and Pull

Do your first catch by pressing the palm of your top hand down. If you are rolling to your right, then your right hand is/will be on top. Bend your arm at the elbow.

Ensure to keep your arm aligned at a downward angle. Your shoulder is at the top, your elbow below that, then your wrist, and finally your fingers at the bottom. Doing this will maximize your first pull.

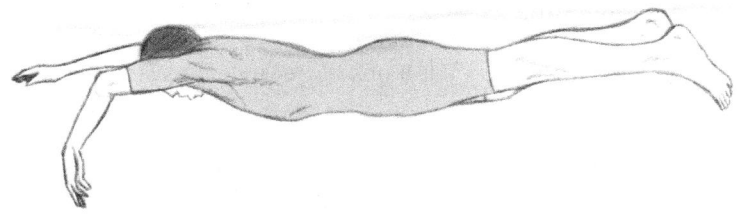

Continue the catch as you rotate onto your side. Your forearm is vertical, elbow above your wrist.

Stay on your side until your recovery stage.

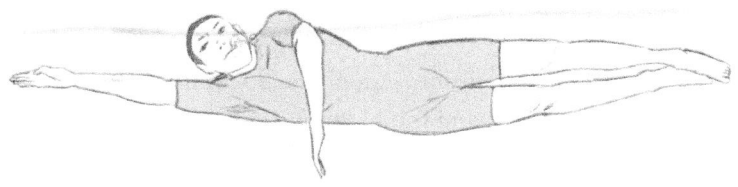

Flow into the pull by continuing the movement of your top arm until your hand is in line with your upper thigh. Your hand follows your midline. Be careful not to raise your elbow too high.

At this stage, your arm is almost fully extended. Do not let your hand come out of the water.

Now is a good time to take a breath. When you exhale, do so in a slow and steady manner.

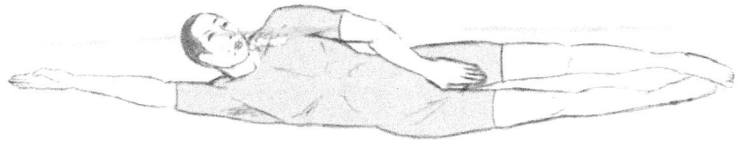

Second Catch and Pull

Start your second catch and pull with your other arm by sweeping it down.

Your palm faces down and stays fixed in that position.

As you sweep down it creates resistance against the water, propelling you forward.

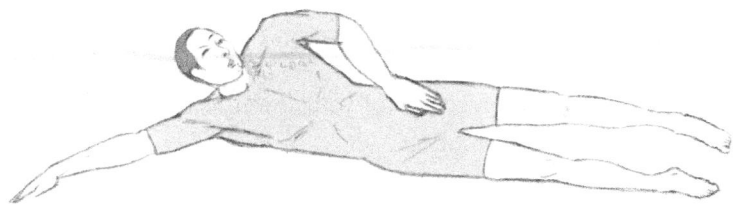

When your arm is vertical, your palm will be facing to your rear.

Continue the arc of your bottom arm until your hand is on your thigh.

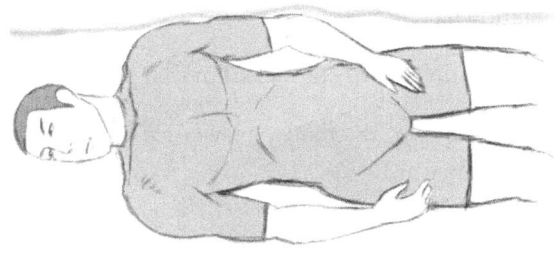

The catch, pull, and recovery of your lower arm is almost identical to a breaststroke motion.

Note: As you do the second pull you can either leave your head up breathing or look back down. If you have a tendency to sink you are better off looking back down.

Recovery

Start the recovery with a simultaneous scissor kick and arm movement.

Bring both your arms up through the center-line of your body. They then travel back into the streamline position, like breaststroke. Keep your arms and hands underwater and as close to your body as possible.

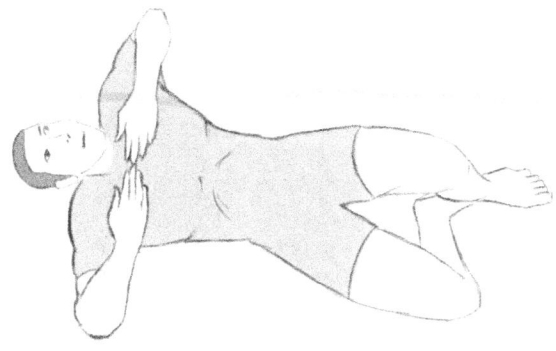

Continue your arms forward past your face as you do the scissor kick. Finish in the streamlined position.

Scissor Kick

Do the scissor kick as you bring your arms forward. This helps with propulsion and corkscrew's your body back into the streamline position.

Move your top leg forward and your bottom leg backward at the same time. Bring them back together in the streamlined position. Keep your toes flexed towards your shin until you adopt the streamlined position.

Draw your top knee up so there is a 90° angle at your hip and knee. At the same time, bend your bottom leg back at the knee.

Extend the lower part of your top leg in front of your torso as you kick your bottom leg back.

Point your toes once you have extended your legs, then draw them into the streamline position.

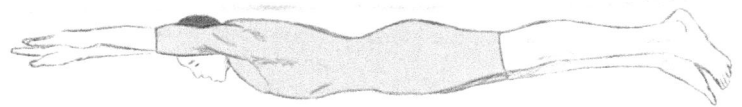

Slowly exhale as you glide in the streamline position. Be sure to get the most out of the glide before starting the next arm cycle.

If speed is more important you can flutter kick before initiating your first pull again. You could also use the sprinter's CSS.

Sprinter's CSS

Use the sprinter's CSS when you need to go faster. The tradeoff is that you will use more energy since will use a greater stroke count over the same distance.

To do the sprinter's CSS do a half stroke on your second pull. Everything else stays the same.

From the start of the second pull, bring your arm down as normal until it is almost at a right angle to your body.

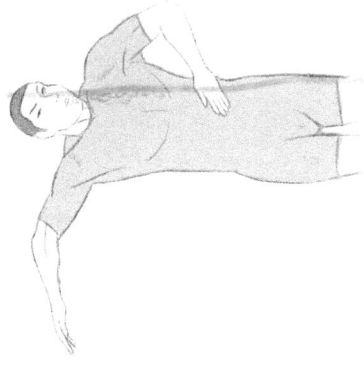

Instead of pulling it all the way to your thigh, scoop it up into your armpit.

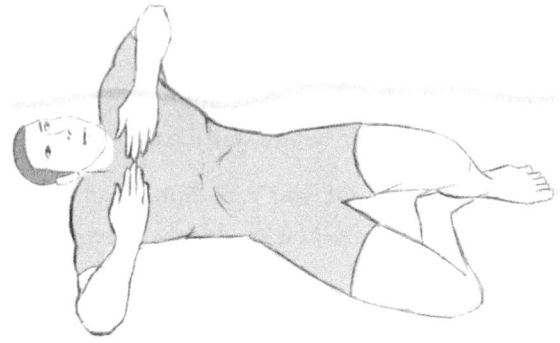

From here, push it forward into a full extension as normal.

Guide Stroke

Use the guide stroke to check your direction when using the CSS to swim a long distance.

It uses a breaststroke-type movement for your arms and the dolphin kick for your legs.

Start in the streamline position.

Push your palms out against the water to a position a little wider than your shoulders.

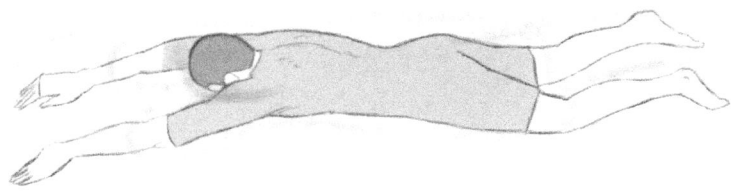

Press your palms against the water as you rotate your hands and lower arms into a vertical position.

Your finger-tips point down and your palms angle toward your chest. Pull your palms towards your chest.

This creates forward propulsion and allows you to raise your head above the surface. Now you can breathe and look around.

Try not to lift your head too far out of the water.

This will cause your hips and legs to sink, which will decrease your momentum.

Recover your arms back to the streamline position as you would with breast-stroke. Keep them close to your body along your centerline.

As you recover your arms, use the downward motion of the dolphin kick. This helps with propulsion back into the streamline position. From here you can continue into CSS or another guide stroke.

Note: For more instruction on the dolphin kick, see the underwater fly-kick chapter.

If you get disorientated, tread water until you figure out which direction you need to swim in.

SWIMMING LONG DISTANCE UNDERWATER

There are two major factors when it comes to swimming long distance underwater:

1. Efficient stroke.
2. Lung capacity (how long you can hold your breath for).

This section is a 5 stage training plan. Use it to increase your ability to swim long distance underwater. The aim is to swim 50 meters underwater.

Important! *Depriving yourself of oxygen is dangerous. Safe training is paramount!*

Safety

Here are some safety pointers when practicing to swim long distance underwater.

- Train with a partner, and not at the same time. Your friend must watch you so he can help if something goes wrong. If you must train alone, then at the very least make sure there is a lifeguard present.
- Stay in shallow water, especially to begin with.
- Never push yourself to beat your last time or distance. Only hold your breath for as much as comfortable. Trying to beat yourself will have an adverse effect anyway. You're much better off staying relaxed and seeing where you "pop-up".
- If you begin to panic at any moment, relax and surface.
- Listen to your body. If you get light headed, your vision

begins to fade, or you get any other abnormal sensation, surface immediately.
- Work on your lung capacity on dry land and concentrate more on efficient stroke when you're in the water.

Stage 1 - Dry Land Breath Holding

Practice holding your breath for longer periods of time while on dry land.

In the Survival Fitness Plan, we use minimal preparation for breath holding. This is so you know how far you can get in emergency situations. Breathe in, breathe out, breathe in, then go.

Take these breaths slowly from deep within your diaphragm. This is to rid your lungs of low-quality air (CO_2).

Tip: You know you're using correct breathing if your belly is moving up and down rather than your shoulders. When your chest and shoulders move it means you're breathing with only the top part of your lungs. This deep breathing is also useful for recovery after a workout.

Here are more detailed instructions for the inhale, exhale, inhale, sequence.

Whilst doing the following, relax your muscles and remain as still and as calm as possible. This includes not "clock watching" which will make you anxious. The more relaxed and still you are, the less oxygen your body will consume.

- Breathe in for a count of 5 seconds, hold it for 1 second, then breathe out for a count of 10 seconds.
- When exhaling, push out every last drop of air, and

push your tongue up against your teeth. This forms a valve which helps to control the release of air. Your breath should make a hissing sound as you exhale.
- Inhale slowly to about 80-85% capacity. Start at the bottom near your diaphragm, then up into your sternum, and finally into your chest.
- Hold your breath for as long as you can, and when you first start to feel the need to breathe, swallow a little spit. This helps to relax your breathing reflex.
- When you need to breathe out, let out little puffs of air at a time.
- When you're finished, push out as much air as possible to get rid of any extra carbon dioxide.

Don't try this sequence again until you get your body back to normal oxygen levels. Breathe steadily for at least 5 minutes and don't do it more than 3 times in a single session. Only do one session a day.

After a few practice sessions try adding in slow movements, such as walking. This will prepare your body to dive and swim with less air.

Stage 2 - Static Underwater Breath Holding

Stage two is the same as stage one, but underwater. The point of this stage is to get you comfortable holding your breath underwater.

Inhale, exhale fully, inhale to 80% capacity, then hold and submerge.

Keep your mouth and nose closed while underwater. Use your fingers to hold your nose shut if you need.

Stay relaxed, and once you are near your limit, resurface. Blow out any extra air as you rise so that you can take a fresh breath immediately.

Stage 3 - Static Apnea Training

In this stage, you will use static apnea training. This conditions your lungs and body to withstand the effects of prolonged breath-holding.

This stage is ongoing. You can move on to stage 4 while doing it.

IMPORTANT: This is a dry land activity. DO NOT try it underwater!

There are two separate programs for static apnea training. One conditions your CO_2 tolerance. The other increases the amount of oxygen your lungs can store.

Each program has its own training table. The recovery stage is when you can breathe — breath normal for the allocated time. During the breath hold stage, hold your breath for the allocated time.

Only start O_2 tolerance training once you can hold your breath for at least 90 seconds.

You can do both CO_2 and O_2 sessions on the same day, but do not do them immediately after one another. Do one in the morning and one at night.

Do not do more than one training session of each per day.

CO2 Tolerance

CO2 tolerance training consists of a series of alternating breath-holds and rest periods. Your breathing time gets less and less while your breath holding stays the same.

Start off with a breath-hold period that you're comfortable with. 50-70% of your capability is good. Add 5 or 10 seconds each day.

This table represents one training session, i.e., you recover and breath hold 8 times.

Use the same breath hold time for each one.

In your next training session (the following day), you increase your breath hold time by 5 or 10 seconds.

#	Recovery	Breath Hold
1	2m 30s	50-70%
2	2m 15s	50-70%
3	2m	50-70%
4	1m 45s	50-70%
5	1m 30s	50-70%
6	1m 15s	50-70%
7	1m	50-70%
8	45s	50-70%

O2 Tolerance

In O2 tolerance training, your recovery period stays the same. Instead, you increase your breath holding.

Only start O2 tolerance training once you can hold your breath for at least 90 seconds.

This table represents one training session.

#	Recovery	Breath Hold
1	2m	50%
2	2m	55%
3	2m	60%
4	2m	65%
5	2m	70%
6	2m	75%
7	2m	80%
8	2m	85%

Additional Ways to Increase your Breath Holding Ability

There are some other things you can do to increase your breath holding ability:

- Exercise often.
- Lose weight (if you are overweight).
- Learn to play a wind or brass instrument.
- Take up singing.
- Don't do drugs, especially smoking!

Body Response Information

*Important! This is for informational purposes. **DO NOT** practice/experiment with it.*

When you hold your breath for an extended period of time your body goes through three response stages.

1. **Convulsions.** When you first get an urge to take a breath and you don't, you will have convulsions in your diaphragm. You can learn to fight through this, and if you do then you will gain a couple of minutes before

you need to breathe.
2. **Spleen Release.** If you fight through the convulsions your spleen responds by releasing oxygen-rich blood. Your body will calm down and you will get a surge of energy. Use this energy to get somewhere that you can breathe!
3. **Blackout.** If you do not find fresh oxygen you will black out, and if you are underwater at the time you will drown.

Stage 4 - Efficient Stroke

This teaches the technique for an efficient underwater stroke. The only aim is to learn the stroke. Don't try to break any underwater distance records.

This stroke uses a combination of a modified breast-stroke (for the arms) and the dolphin kick. Do it as one fluid motion.

Start off in a streamlined glide and stay in it for as long as possible.

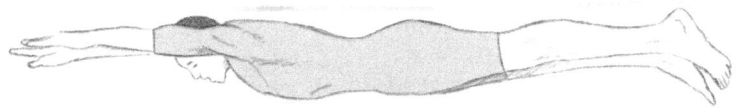

When you are almost to a complete stop, turn your palms out and separate your hands. Do the out-sweep of the breast-stroke. Use webbed finger as described in the freestyle chapter (under the heading Catch). Allow your legs to float up, the higher the better. Keep your head down.

Survival Swimming

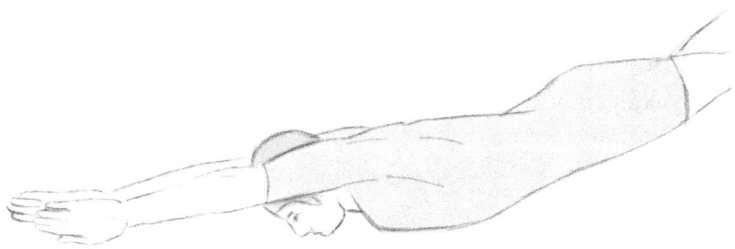

As you do the breaststroke arm movement, arch your body extending your back and shoulders. You aim is to make your body like a spring which you will snap down to propel you forward.

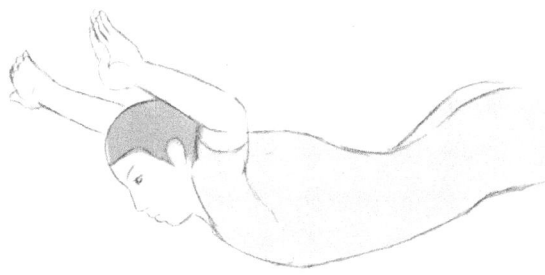

Bring your arms and forearms into a vertical position, elbows facing up. Snap your arms and legs down together.

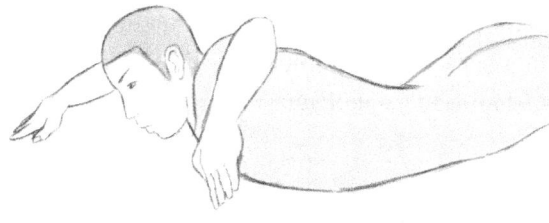

Your legs/torso do a dolphin kick. Your arms go into a double arm pull stroke by pushing against the water down along your body. Remember your webbed fingers.

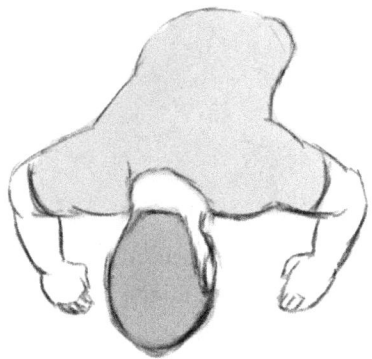

Keep your arms vertical for as long as you can and end in a streamline position with your arms by your sides. Glide in this position for as long as you can.

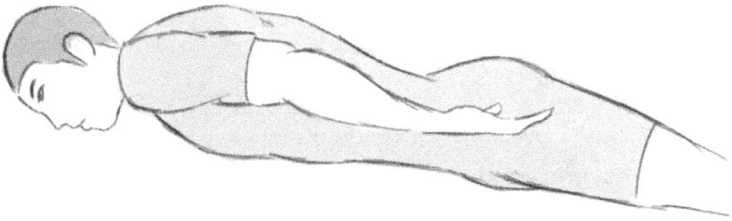

Do a standard breaststroke frog kick. At the same time bring your hands back into the streamline glide you started in, with your arms/hands in front of you.

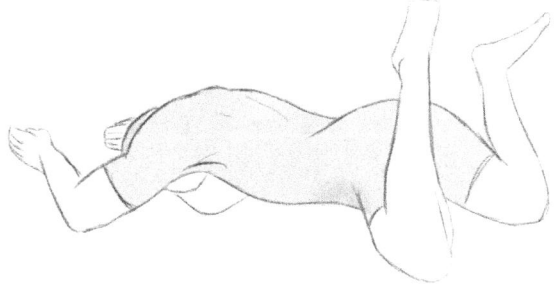

Repeat this sequence. When you start to run out of breath go into your preferred surface stroke. CSS or freestyle is best.

Stage 5 - 50m Swim: Revise the safety pointers from the start of this chapter!

Before attempting this final stage, you should be able to:

- Swim 25 meters underwater in under 30 seconds and using 5 strokes or less.
- Hold your breath for at least 90 seconds while walking on dry land.

The first part of stage 5 is to build up your breath holding ability while moving on dry land.

Hold your breath while doing SFP Super-Burpees for a minute. When you can do 6 in a minute you are ready to attempt the 50-meter underwater swim.

WATER SAFETY, SELF-RESCUE, AND SURVIVAL

Being near any body of water has its inherent dangers, and open water has even more. This section has information on the different dangers in various forms of open water. It explains what to do when faced with these dangers, covering self-rescue and survival in solo and group scenarios.

In this manual, the term "open water" refers to any natural body of water such as oceans, lakes, and rivers.

PROTECTIVE CLOTHING

Protect yourself from cold and injuries with the appropriate clothing.

Keeping Warm

Being hot outside does not mean it will be warm in the water. It only takes a slight change of weather to take the situation from fun to dangerous.

- Be prepared with the right clothing and use layering.
- Choose fabrics that provide warmth even when wet. Not cotton or jeans.
- In colder conditions, use a wetsuit.
- Once out of the water, put on warm clothes. Use clothing that blocks the wind, such as a poncho.

Layering

Layering means using several items of thin clothing as opposed to one or two thick ones. If you get too warm you can strip one or two layers without losing all your protection.

There are three basic layers. Base, insulator and outer.

Base Layer

The first layer, (base layer), will reduce water flowing past your skin and is also good for sun protection. You want a skin-tight, quick-drying material that will wick the water away. Rash vests are a good example. Polypropylene, polyester, and lycra are good materials for your base layer.

Insulating Layer

The insulating layer keeps you warm when it gets colder. It should fit snug. Not too tight or too loose. Use materials that dry fast. Unlined tracksuits work well, as does wool and fleece. Unlined is important, otherwise, it will hold air and water. A hooded top helps to prevent heat from escaping through your head. It also provides sun protection.

Adjust the number of insulating layers you use depending on the temperature. In warmer climates, you may not even need one.

Outer Layer

Your outer layer should be a water and windproof shell. Its purpose is to keep you warm and the elements (such as wind and rain) out. You will still get wet, either from perspiration or from being in the water.

A rain jacket, an anorak or a light nylon over-all works well. It should be large enough so you have good freedom of movement. This will also trap a warm layer of air inside it.

Being windproof is very important for the outer layer.

Other Considerations

Footwear

Footwear is especially important in unknown waters where your feet may get injured. Simple canvas shoes with drain holes work well. Wear ones that are easy to remove in case you get caught in rocks.

Wearing socks provides insulation and also prevents chafing.

Swimming in footwear, as with any clothing, will create extra drag. Experiment with it during training.

Goggles

Swimming goggles, or a mask, are not essential but are useful if you want to see underwater.

It is a good idea to always wear goggles in a chlorinated/chemical pool.

Poncho

A poncho is an excellent all-around piece of survival equipment. When it comes to water training, you will use ponchos for some self-rescue exercises. It can also become an improvised shelter or emergency blanket (extra warmth) when not in the water.

Visibility

Being visible in the water is for safety and survival. You want to be easy to spot by any water traffic. Also, if you get in trouble you will be easier to find by rescue services.

Maintenance

Always wash yourself and all your gear in fresh water after training in any type of water. This will keep everything in the best working condition for as long as possible.

Rinsing your gear under a tap is not enough. Most of the bad stuff (salt, chemicals, etc.) will not get washed out. It is best to wear it in the shower or put it in the washing machine.

Restrictions

The more clothes you have on the harder it will be to swim. The best way to prepare is to simulate falling into the water while clothed and then swimming to safety.

Water-logged clothes will also make climbing out of the water harder.

SAFE ENTRY TECHNIQUES

There are a variety of ways to enter the water. The methods described in this section focus on safety and are also used in rescue situations.

Always enter shallow or unknown waters feet first. Unknown waters are when you are unsure of the water depth, and/or if you can't see what lays beneath the surface.

Wade Entry

When possible, the wade entry is the best way to enter unknown waters.

It is walking into the water very carefully. Feel your way forward with your feet until the water is chest deep, then start to swim.

Slide Entry

Use the slide entry for shallow or unknown waters with a steep angled edge, such as a pool edge. It is also useful in crowded areas since it is easier to control than other entry methods.

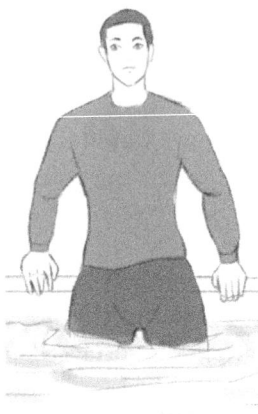

The slide entry is very simple. Sit down with your feet/legs hanging down into (or above) the water. Use your hands to slide yourself into the water.

For shallow waters, once your feet are firm, continue forward using the wade entry.

If speed is a factor and you plan to push off the wall once you are in the water, don't push too hard during the slide entry.

If you are too far away from the edge you won't be able to do a good push off, which is where your initial propulsion comes from.

Step-off Entry

When entering shallow or unknown waters, and you are too high for a slide entry, use the step-off.

Step off your platform into the water.

Keep your knees flexed and be ready to absorb any impact in case you hit the floor.

You can then wade or swim depending on the situation.

Stride Entry

Only use the stride entry when you know the water is at least 1.5 meters deep, and the slide entry is not appropriate.

One of the big advantages of the stride entry is that you keep your head above the water. This means you can keep your sight on something, such as a drowning victim.

Put your arms out to your sides and step one foot out in front of you. Planted your foot well so you don't slip. Keep looking at your target the whole time.

Look up a little as you lean forward into the water.

Slap your hands down as you hit the water. Looking up and slapping down helps to keep your head above the water.

High-Level Entry

This is good to use when you have to enter the water from a height of 3+ meters. You must be sure that the water depth is appropriate for the height you are jumping from. Also ensure that your landing zone is a large enough area-wise, i.e., length and width.

Unlike all the previous entry methods, the high-level entry is not safe to do while carrying gear. If you have a backpack or anything else, throw it in before jumping.

Consider wearing long clothing as it will help protect your body.

Take a large breath and jump away from the surface. You don't want to hit anything on the way down.

Cross your ankles and place your hands in fists in front of your thighs. This puts your arms down and close to your body.

Bend your knees a little.

Look straight ahead at the horizon and arch your back. Looking down or up will cause you to lean forward or back respectively. Arching your back will help keep you straight. You want to hit the water as vertical and straight as possible.

Allow your knees to flex once you hit the water. This will help slow you down.

Height vs Water Depth

The higher your jumping-off platform, the deeper the water needs to be.

The best way to judge is if you have seen others do it, and even then you must be very careful.

Note: All these calculations are only approximate so it is easy to do them in your head. The results are good enough to use.

Start with at least 2.5 meters (m) of water depth. If you're jumping from higher than 1.5 m you need to add an extra 0.6 m of depth for every 3 m increase in height.

Calculating Height

A simple but effective way to calculate your height from the water is to drop something into it. Any solid object that won't catch air will work, like a rock. Time how long it takes to hit the water.

Multiply that number by itself, and then multiply that answer by 16, i.e., $(x^2) \times 16$.

This gives you the approximate height in feet. Multiply it by 0.3 to convert it into meters.

Calculating Water Depth

Get a long stick (or something similar) and put it in the water until it hits the floor. Measure how much of it got wet.

This is easy in theory but hard in practice.

SURVIVAL SWIMMING STYLES

In order to successfully overcome obstacles in the water you need to adjust your swimming style depending on the situation and what lays ahead.

The Defensive Position

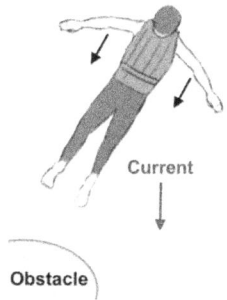

In most cases, the best thing to do when experiencing trouble in the water is to tread water and signal for help. When in swift water treading may not be practical as the current will drag you away.

In this case, the best thing to do is adopt the defensive position.

Get on your back with your feet up so you can see your toes. Float downstream feet first.

This position will enable you to see the path ahead. Guide yourself through the safest route of passage.

If you meet any obstructions, absorb the impact with your legs.

Keeping your feet up ensures they don't get caught in obstructions beneath the surface.

Never try to stand up in river rapids that are deep enough for you to float in.

When you see an obstruction you want to avoid, angle your body so that your feet point towards the obstacle. Aim the top of your head towards your destination and use a modified sculling motion to get there.

The Aggressive Position

If you see an opportunity to get to safety, and it is deep enough to do so, you can use an aggressive position to get there. The aggressive position is doing freestyle while keeping your head out of the water.

The aggressive position is very tiring so reserve it for when you need short bursts of power. You could also use breast or side stroke. They will be slower but with better visibility.

WAVES

By being able to identify the types of waves you can make the best decision about whether it is safe to swim in them or not. There are three basic types of waves to look for. Spilling, plunging, and surging.

Spilling Waves

A spilling wave is when the crest of the wave tumbles down its front. If the sandbank it breaks on is shallow it will form a "tube".

Spilling waves occur on ocean floors with a gradual slope. They are most common with onshore winds (winds that blow across the ocean towards land). They break for longer and in a gentle fashion when compared to other waves.

They are the safest types of waves to swim in.

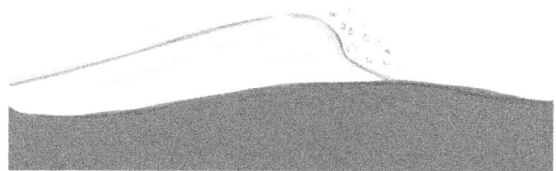

Plunging Waves

Plunging waves occur when the beach slope is moderate to steep or if it has a sudden change in depth, e.g., a reef or sandbar. They usually occur with offshore winds (winds that blow across the land towards the ocean) and at low tide.

These waves become more vertical than spilling waves and break with much more force. Experienced surfers often enjoy them for the "tube" they may create.

Plunging waves have a lot more potential to cause serious injury to the swimmer. It is best to not swim in them.

If caught in a plunging wave, hug your knees and roll up into a ball.

Surging Waves

Surging waves occur when long period swells meet steep beach slopes. The bottom of the wave is fast enough that the crest never forms.

As a result, there is little sign of breaking/whitewash.

Surging waves are dangerous. Although the wave break is minimal, the force of the wave is still powerful. They can knock you over and then drag you out to sea.

Do not to swim when there are surging waves.

Although not waves, another thing to be aware of is rough or choppy water. Rough seas can quickly drain your energy. It is best to get out and wait until the water is calm again.

Riding Waves to Shore

When the waves are not too large you can use them to carry you to shore. Choose your wave and swim forward with it. Before it breaks dive down a little so the break goes over you.

Large Waves

With larger surf, it is better to swim towards shore between oncoming waves. As a wave approaches, face it and go under water until it has passed over you. Swim towards the shore as much as you can before repeating the process with the next wave.

You may get caught in the undertow of a large wave. Get to the surface to avoid getting dragged out too far.

Rocky Shores

Only try to land on rocky shores if there is no other option. It is better to do a long distance swim to an easier landing point than it is to risk injury on rocky shores.

When you have to land on a rocky shore you must choose a safe landing point. Avoid where the waves crash into the rocks with a high white spray. Instead, aim for where the waves rush up onto rocks.

Once you know where you want to land, approach slowly. Use a large wave to carry you in. Get into the defensive position so you can absorb the impact.

If you do not reach the shore on the first wave, swim in the aggressive position with your hands only. When the next wave approaches, re-adopt the defensive position.

When you climb up the rocks keep your knees a little bent and your feet close together.

TIDES AND CURRENTS

Tides

Tide refers to the rising and falling of the sea. High tide is when the water is at its highest level, and low tide is when it is at its lowest level.

A few different natural forces influence tidal characteristics. It is important to check the tidal times depending on where and when you plan to visit the beach.

The change of water level due to tides can completely change the landscape within a short period of time. For example, if you walk out to a land mass in the morning, in the afternoon the path that you used may be underwater.

Currents

Current refers to the constant flow of water. It is always there and it acts differently depending on many factors. These include water volume, channel width, gradient, weather, obstructions, etc.

Although you can use water currents in your favor, they can also take you where you do not want to go. Even slow ones can knock a person off his feet and carry him out to sea/downstream.

Currents are usually slower along the inside bend of rivers opposed to the outside bend. Also, currents are faster on the surface of the water.

Rip Currents

Rip currents can occur near beaches with breaking waves. They are strong currents which drag swimmers out to sea. Generally, the larger the waves, the stronger the rip current will be.

Signs of a Rip Current

The following characteristics can indicate a rip current:

- A channel of rippled water (more-so than the surrounding water)
- Dark water (indicates greater depth)
- Debris and/or sea-foam moving in a steady line out to sea.
- Different colored water beyond the breaking waves.
- Murky water (indicates disturbed sand by the rip)
- Waves breaking further out to sea on both sides of the rip.

Look for a channel of water that is different (calmer or choppier) than the water surrounding it.

A rip current may also be present with none of these characteristics showing.

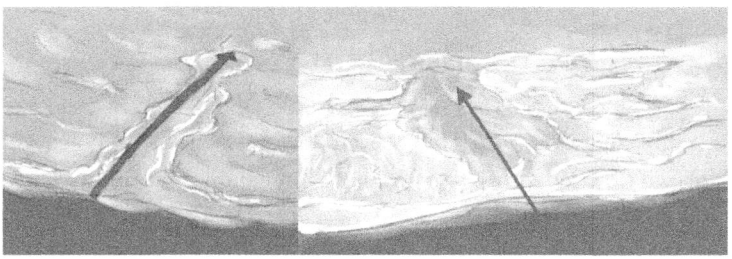

Escaping the Rip Current

- Do not try to swim against it!
- Stay calm
- Swim parallel to the shore until you reach the breaking waves zone, then swim back to shore.
- If you can't escape it, conserve your energy (float or tread water) and signal for help.

In this picture, the thin arrows show the direction of the current. The 4 thicker arrows are your channels of escape.

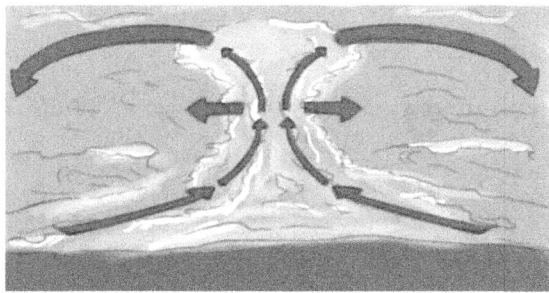

OBSTRUCTIONS

An obstruction is anything in the water which changes the normal flow (current) of the water. Almost anything in the water will do this, such as rocks, branches, etc.

There are specific techniques to use depending on the obstruction you come across.

Drops

A drop is when water drops straight down. A waterfall is an obvious example.

Never go in the water upstream from a drop. Even if the water is shallow and appears calm before the drop, it is still very dangerous.

When going over a drop is unavoidable, ball up and try to land feet first. Landing feet first is best to protect your head. Balling up will lessen the possibility of getting caught in a foot entrapment.

If it is a high drop, as you go over the edge adopt the high-level entry position.

Eddies

Eddies occur when water rushes around obstacles and the current comes back on itself. They are often a safe-haven since the water in the eddy is generally calmer.

The barrier of separation between the upstream and downstream water is the eddy line. Problems can occur when crossing this line, especially if the flow is fast. Unless you are in a craft that can capsize (like a kayak) you shouldn't face much danger.

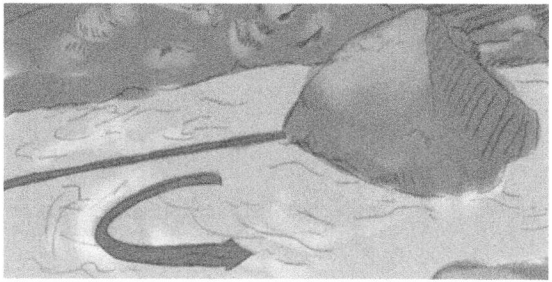

You can break through the eddy line with barrel rolls.

As you approach the eddy, place your closest hand into the upstream moving water inside it.

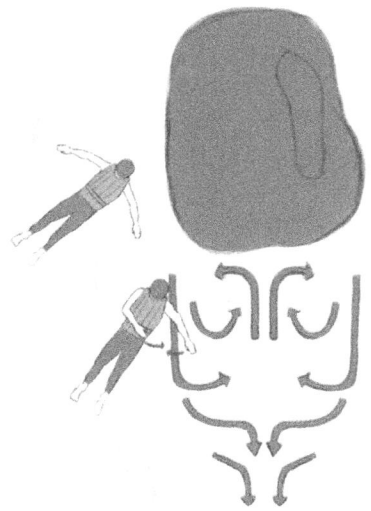

Scoop the water with this hand as you roll over onto your stomach. You are now in the aggressive swimming position.

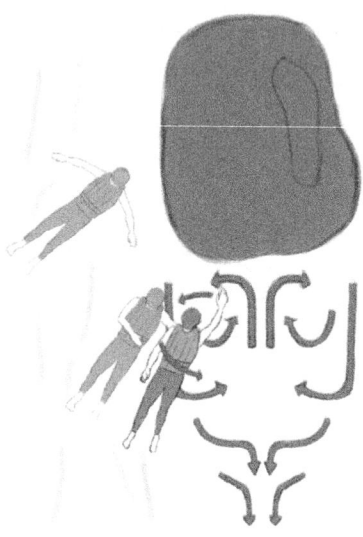

Continue to roll until you are back in the defensive swimming position.

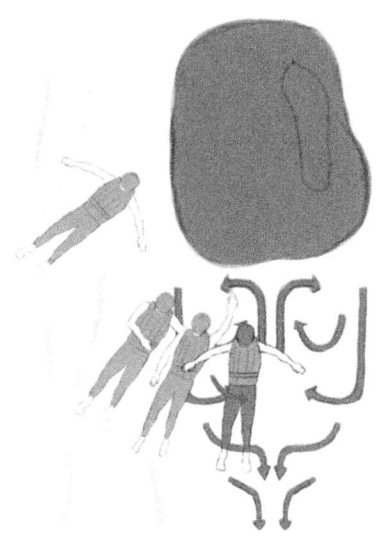

You may need to barrel roll a few times to get into the eddy. You can finish in either the defensive or aggressive swimming position.

This image is a demonstration of using defensive and aggressive swimming to get out of a river.

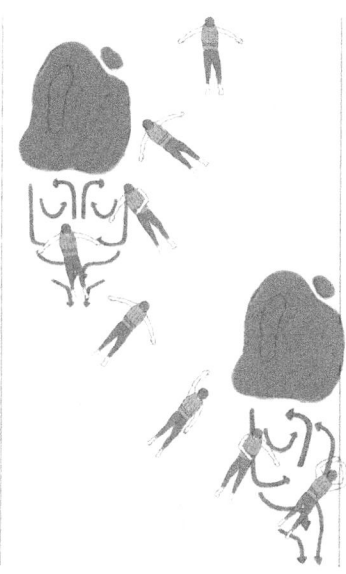

Sometimes an eddy can create a whirlpool effect. This is when eddies become dangerous since the whirlpool can suck you down. In this case, you should stay clear of them.

Entrapments

An entrapment is anything that you can get snagged on, e.g., your clothing snagging on a branch underwater.

To prevent this, make sure all your gear and clothing is a snug fit.

A foot entrapment is when you get your foot stuck. It is very dangerous as the force of the water can hold you under.

Holes

Holes occur when water flows over a ledge (such as a rock). This creates a hydraulic flow (water circulating on top of itself) which can trap things. It is like a vertical eddy and is very dangerous.

Dams and dam-like structures (weirs, spillways, ledges) have severe hydraulic action. Keep away from their downstream base.

If caught in a hole you need to relax and swim out the bottom (where the slower current flows out) or to the side.

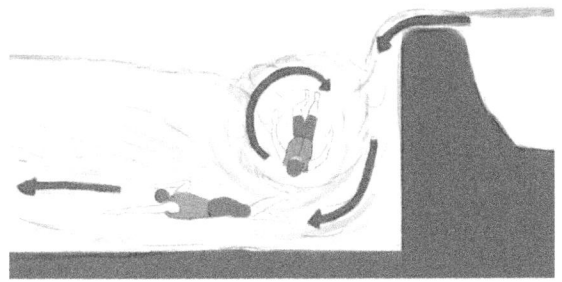

Pillows

When a rock is close to the waters surface the water hits the top of it, forcing it upwards. This creates a "pillow" of water downstream of the rock.

The more submerged a rock is, the further downstream the pillow will be. If the rock is very close to the surface the pillow will be right on top of it. With enough experience, you will be able to tell when a rock is close to the surface or not by the type of pillow it creates.

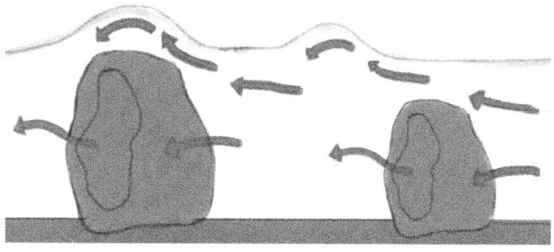

If the rock is out of the water, the pillow becomes a cushion. This is due to the water flowing up against it. When the current is strong enough, it may form a series of compression waves.

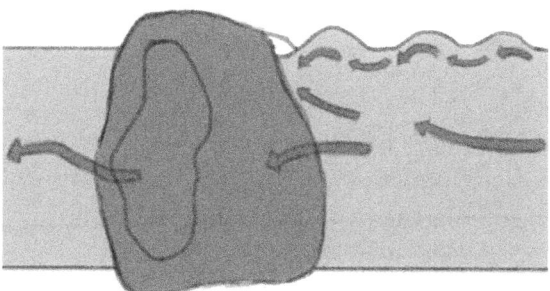

Rapids

A rapid is a turbulent section of water created by faster flowing water over obstacles, such as rocks. These obstacles may or may not break the water's surface. This faster water is due to an increased gradient and/or a constriction in the channel.

To negotiate a rapid, look for a downstream "V" in the water (the bottom of the V pointing downstream). This indicates an unobstructed flow of water. In most cases, it will be the preferred path of passage.

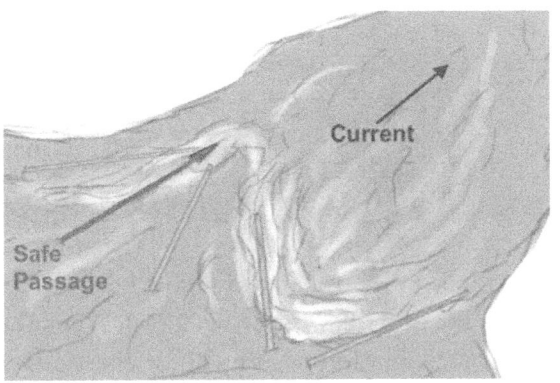

Rocks

Apart from being a cause for other types of obstructions, the rock itself can present danger. Avoid these obstructions altogether by entering the water downstream of them.

Walking on slippery rocks (or any slippery surface) near water is never a good idea.

Rocks under the water's surface can become foot entrapments. It is very dangerous and is one of the main reasons to keep your feet up in the defensive position.

When in the water heading towards a rock, use the defensive position as described before.

If you get pinned up against a rock, lean downstream to get loose.

Rocks are not all bad. They may serve as a lifeline to hold onto. They can also create eddies which can be safe havens in turbulent waters.

Sweepers and Strainers

Strainers are objects in the water that allow water to pass through them but not objects. They can be natural like branches, or artificial such as wire fences.

A sweeper is a strainer that hangs low over or into the water.

Both of these things can impede your safe passage, and they often double as entrapments.

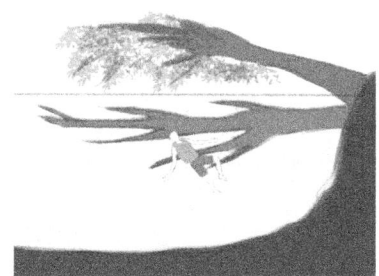

When swimming into a strainer is unavoidable, maneuver into the aggressive swimming position. Swim hard to launch yourself up and onto (or over) the obstruction.

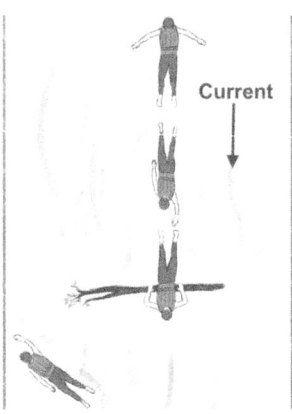

When forced below the surface swim downstream using your hands in front of you to part the branches.

If your legs get tangled in long weeds swim downstream using only your arms.

Like friendly rocks, sometimes sweepers (not strainers) can serve as a lifeline. You might be able to use them to climb to shore.

Undercut Rocks

An undercut rock is one where the water flows below it as opposed to around. The water's current can drag the swimmer underneath it and pin him there.

Normal river features acting strangely are good indications of an undercut rock, e.g.,

- The pillow or cushion is missing
- There is a boil (where the water is not flowing down or upstream) on the downstream side of the obstacle.

- The eddy has weak (or missing) lines and/or an abnormal current flow.

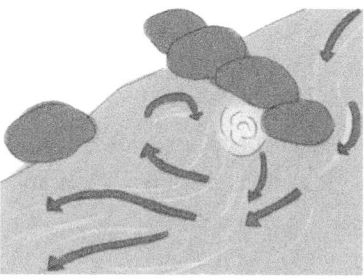

Water Debris

Water debris is anything floating in the water. It can be either natural or unnatural, such as seaweed, logs, trash, etc.

Keep an eye out for these things and avoid them as they can become entrapments.

If there is a lot of debris, such as lots of seaweed, try to avoid it. If you must go through it then crawl over the top by grasping at it with overhand movements. When you are in a group put the strongest person first. He will create a path through the debris for the others to follow.

Manmade pools created behind dams often have many stumps lying below the surface. This is due to the cutting of trees before the flooding of the lowlands.

People

Other people can be a hazard, although more often they are a good thing in a survival situation.

When in open water there are more recreational hazards.

Surfers, jet-skis, boats, etc. Stay away from areas in which these activities take place. If available, use the designated swimming areas instead.

Pollution

Another by-product of people is pollution. Water systems are often used as a dumping ground for all sorts of human and industrial waste.

Swimming in polluted waters may not have an immediate effect, but it could result in illness later.

RIVER CROSSINGS

When crossing a body of water with no bridge you need to use river crossing techniques. They will give you the best chance of making it to the other side unharmed.

Choosing Where to Cross

It is very important to find a safe crossing point before attempting to cross. When practical (and not dangerous), it is best to scout the river from an elevated perspective.

Unless you can jump it, narrow is not best. Look for straight, wide, and shallow water. Current is faster at the bends and usually deeper in narrow channels. Lots of debris is also a sign of fast flow. Test the current by throwing a branch in and seeing how fast it goes.

Although it may be wider, where a river breaks into channels is usually a good crossing location. The energy of the current dissipates and there may be small patches of land where you can take breaks.

Mild ripples are generally safe to cross. Whitecaps (small, surface breaking waves) will be slippery.

Also, check downstream 100 meters of where you plan to cross. Make sure there are not any hazards that you could get swept into.

Consider your entry and exit points. An easy exit point is especially important. You want something low and open so you don't have to climb through or up anything.

You may be able to avoid getting wet if you find a fallen log that spans the width of the river. If you do find one, don't try to walk over it. It is much safer to straddle it and scoot yourself across. You must be very sure it will hold your weight. When you are in a group, only cross one person at a time.

Wading

Wading is a method of walking through water. Use it solo or in a group to cross water no deeper than thigh height.

You can take your pants, shirt, and socks off to lessen the waters drag. Doing this also gives you dry clothes on the other side.

Keep your shoes on. You don't want to risk damaging your feet and they will also give you more traction.

Tie your clothing to the top of your pack or in one bundle if you don't have a pack. The idea is to keep everything together so it is easier to find if you have to discard them while crossing.

If wading across with a pack, waterproof the contents. Carry it well upon your shoulders. Leave your waist belt unclipped and loosen your shoulder straps so you can discard it if needed. You will not want to be struggling to get it off if the current sweeps you off your feet.

Don't worry about having a heavy pack when crossing. It will keep you more stable.

Waterproofing Your Pack

A waterproofed pack will not only keep all your kit dry, it can also be an effective flotation device.

Double waterproof everything at the very least.

Line your pack with a large, tough, plastic bag. If you don't want to buy a pack liner, then you can use a dead-dog bag from the vet. Even a large, tough, plastic trash bag will work.

Group your things into separate, smaller dry-sacks before putting them in your pack. You could use plastic bags and/or zip-locks.

Seal all the bags watertight by following the manufacturer's directions.

For generic plastic bags use the twist and fold method. Leave enough space at the top so you can put several twists in the bag. Fold the twisted part down over itself and secure it with some twine.

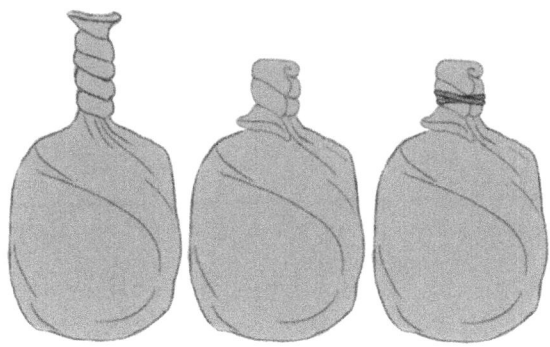

It may be faster to line your pack with two large bags but using this method works better. It means you can access one group of things without having to expose everything else to the elements.

Solo Wading

When wading alone, use a strong branch to support you as you cross. Three legs are far more stable than two.

Position yourself upstream of your chosen exit point so that you can cross at a 45° angle to the current.

Face upstream and place the tip of your branch on the bottom of the river in front of you. Have it well slanted and let the current push it against your shoulder. Your branch breaks the current and provides stability. Shuffle sideways and a little downstream across the river. Use small, low, steps. Do not cross your feet.

Always maintain at least two points of contact with the bottom of the river. Don't move too far on either side of your branch. You do not want to be leaning.

Only reposition the branch once your feet are very stable on the river floor. Shift it in small increments feeling for your next placement. Lift it off the river floor only as much as you need to.

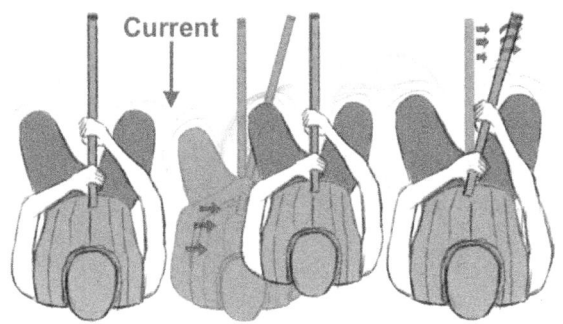

Group Wading

When two or more people need to get across you can use group wading. The technique differs a little depending on how many people you have.

For two people wading, the stronger person is upstream, and he faces downstream. The second person faces the first person (looking upstream).

Grab each other by the shoulder straps of each other's life jackets. If you don't have lifejackets, grab t-shirts or upper arms.

One person stays stationary while the other moves. Use the same small sideways steps as explained. Next, the other moves and the first person stays still. Repeat this process.

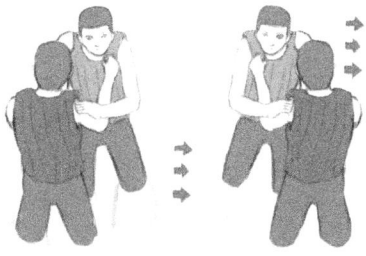

For three to five people, huddle together and each person grabs the people on either side of him. One or more people stay stationary while the rest move. Due to the group formation, you may end up rotating the group around the stationary person/people. It is okay to do this.

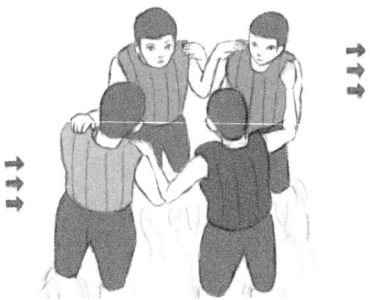

Wading in groups larger than five is not recommended as it becomes too hard to coordinate.

As with all group co-ordination activities, clear communication is very important. Agree on a plan of movement beforehand and appoint one person to direct it as you go.

Inline Crossing

Use inline crossing to move larger numbers of inexperienced people.

With this method, you use your bodies to redirect the current so people can move behind each-other.

The strongest person enters the water facing upstream. The second person moves behind the first. He takes up his position immediately to the side of the first person. They link arms.

Everyone else copies this action until they form one line across the water. More than one person can move at a time.

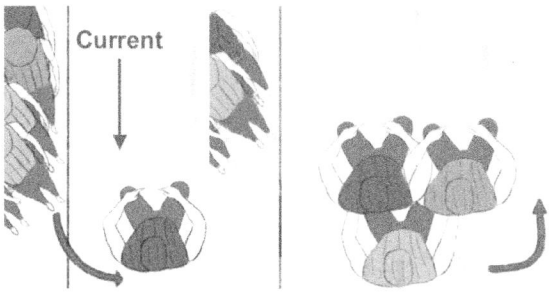

Once the line is steady, the first person moves down it to take his new position at the end.

Everyone does this in the order that they entered. Continue to do this until the line reaches the other side and everyone is on shore.

Rope Crossings

Having a rope increases safety when crossing water and may also increase the speed.

This information assumes you only have rope and no other specialist equipment.

Looped Rope Crossing

This is one of the safest ways to cross a river when you have a rope but no other special equipment. You need at least three people and a rope three times the width of the river.

The first and last people to cross should be the strongest in the group, with the stronger of the two going first.

Tie the rope into a large loop and secure the person who is going to cross first (person A) to the loop. You can tie a loop in the rope and put it over his/her chest.

As person A crosses the other two people let the rope out as needed. They must do their best to keep the rope out of the water and be ready to haul person A back if needed.

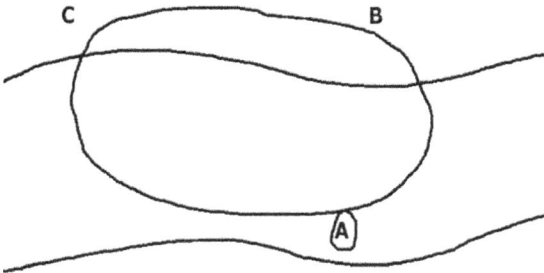

Person A is the only one secured to the rope.

When person A reaches the other side he unties himself.

As many people as needed can now cross (B), one at a time, by securing themselves to the rope and crossing over.

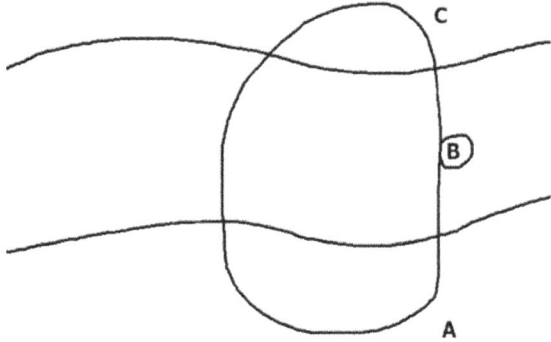

Extra people can help while others are crossing, but person A takes most of the strain. This person should be as close as possible to the position across from the person crossing.

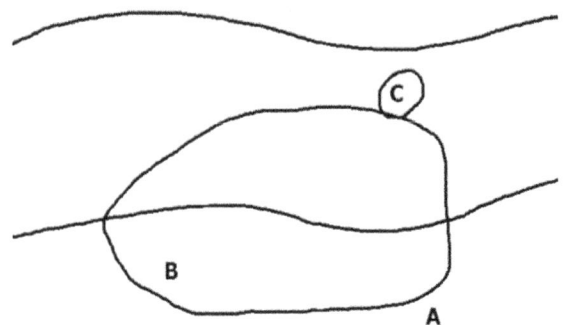

Line Crossing

When you don't have enough rope and/or people to do the looped rope crossing, you can use the line crossing.

Stretch the rope across the water and secure it on both ends. To do this you must get one end of the rope across the other side of the river.

If there is already someone on the other side, you can throw it over. If not, you can attach one end of the rope to the strongest swimmer (or wader) in the group and have him take it over.

It is preferable not to attach the rope directly to the swimmer, e.g., attach it to the back of his life vest instead. That way it will be easier for the swimmer to discard the line if needed.

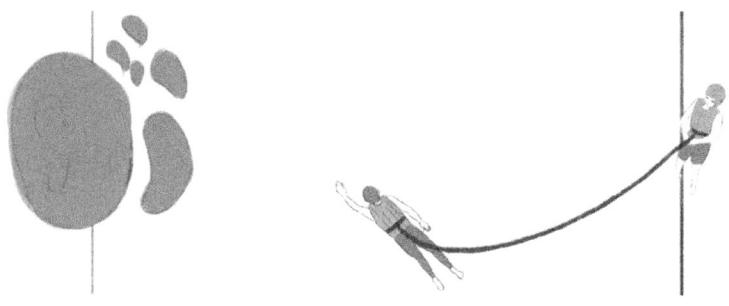

If you must attach the rope directly to the swimmer you can use a bowline.

One person should feed the line out as the swimmer crosses. When feeding the line out, let it drift in the current to reduce drag on the swimmer.

Note: More information on swimming across is in the Swimming Across chapter.

To secure the rope tie it to a sturdy tree, rock, or something similar. If nothing else is available, you can use a human anchor. When doing so, is best to have at least one other person pushing down on him so he doesn't get dragged into the water.

Once the rope is secure on both sides, people can start wading across. Wade across facing the current, using the rope for support. Apply tension to the line by leaning back a little. This will help keep you stable.

Do not cross your legs as you wade across and only move one foot at a time.

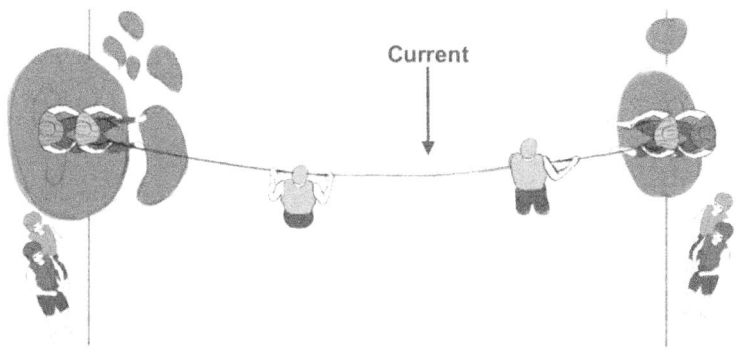

To keep the rope, the last person must release the knot and then attach himself to it.

The people on the other side can pull him across if needed.

Throwing Rope

Before you can do the line crossing you need to get one end of it secured to the other side of the water. Knowing the correct way to throw rope will increase the distance you can throw it.

When throwing rope, in most cases you should aim to over-throw it.

If you intend to keep one end of the rope (which is usually the case) be sure to secure it to something.

Note: Even when throwing all the rope to someone it is a good idea to secure one end. If your throw does not make it over the obstacle you can pull it back. If it does make it then un-secure your end and your friend can pull it over.

Tie a weight or a bulky stopper knot to the end you are going to throw over.

Coil half the rope on the palm of your right hand. Coil the rest of it on your fingers.

Stand on one end to secure it, or tie it to something. Grab the coils you made on your fingers with your left hand.

As you throw release the right-hand coil a split second before the left.

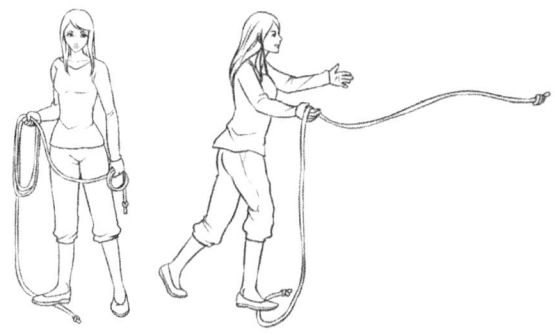

When throwing a weighted rope over a branch beware of it swinging back.

Improvised Raft Building

If the water body you want to cross is too wide, deep, cold, and/or contains dangerous animals, it is a good idea to build a raft. It also helps for keeping you and your gear dry.

Building a raft can be very helpful, but if you do it wrong the results can be disastrous.

Build the raft near to the water in which you want to launch it.

Improvised rafts are not suitable for the ocean. It is unlikely that they will stand up to the force of an angry sea.

There are many ways to build a raft. You can use bamboo, un-rotted wood, or other floating objects.

Always test your raft before committing to using it.

Note: See the bonus chapters for instructions on making cord and knot tying.

Brush Raft

If you have a couple of poncho's in your group, you can construct a brush raft. When done right it can float over 100 kilograms, which is good for one average sized person and his kit.

A tarpaulin (groundsheet) or something similar also works. As long as it is impermeable (waterproof) and about the same size as a poncho.

Spread one poncho on the ground with the inner side facing the sky. Tie a length of cord (vines work) at each corner and also one in the center of each side. Each line must be long enough to reach the opposite diagonal or side. If there isn't dedicated tie points (grommets) then you can bunch up the material in a package around a small rock. Tie a clove hitch below the rock. The rock prevents the knot from slipping off.

Pile fresh, green brush on top of the poncho about half a meter high. It must be all brush, no thick branches or anything that could pierce the ponchos.

Next, find two small saplings and construct an x-frame. Place this x-frame on top of the brush.

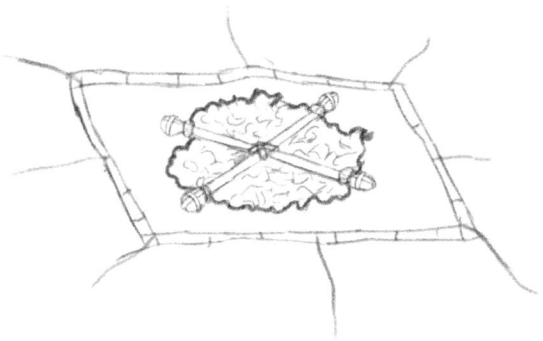

Pile another 50 cm of brush on top of that. Push down on it all to compress it a little.

Pull the sides of the poncho up and around the brush and then tie all the lines together with their opposites. Tie them very secure.

Spread the second poncho on the ground next to your brush package, the inner side facing the sky. Tie cord at the corners and the sides in the same way as the first time. Place your brush package onto the second poncho with the tied side facing down.

Secure it in the same manner. When you place the brush raft in the water, do it with the tied side of the second poncho facing up.

Pressure Raft

A pressure raft takes a lot more effort to build than the brush raft. The tradeoff is that it is much sturdier and can support much more weight.

It is best to use dry, dead, standing trees for logs. Also, not all wood floats. Test the species you intend to use before constructing the raft.

Collect logs of approximately the same diameter and make them the same length. These are your base logs.

How many base logs you collect depends on how wide you want the raft.

Also, gather four logs of thinner diameter. Have them about one meter longer than the thickness of the raft. These are your pressure logs.

Lay two pressure logs on the ground at a distance apart about one meter less than the length of the base logs.

Lay the base logs on top of the pressure logs so that they are perpendicular to them. The ends should have enough overhang so they cannot slip off.

Place the other two pressure bars on top of the thicker ones.

Make them in alignment and parallel with the pressure bars on the bottom.

Lash the ends of the top and bottom pressure bars together at all corners so they "clamp" the raft together. Do it as tight as you can.

Bamboo Raft

Bamboo is one of the best materials for raft building. It is strong, flexible, and floats well.

Note: Bamboo that has not dried out can sink. It can take a while for it to dry out if it is fresh cut.

Cut thick-ish bamboo in 3-meter lengths. If it is too hard to cut down, you can burn it at its base until it falls. Make a hole in the lower sections before burning it to prevent it from exploding.

Make holes in each of the lengths about 30 cm from the ends and also in the center. Make sure the holes will be in alignment when you put the lengths side by side.

Place the bamboo side by side until you get your desired width. Pass a sapling through all the holes.

Create a second row, in the same manner, using one less length of bamboo. Place this second row on top of the first with the lengths of the top row sitting in the valleys of the first.

Lash the lengths of bamboo together, top and bottom and side by side. Also lash the saplings together.

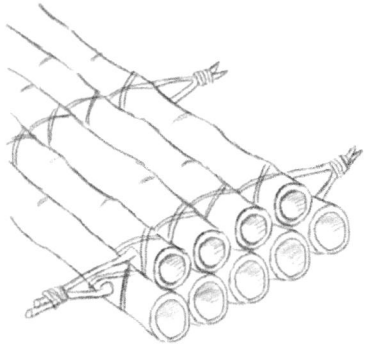

You can do this with materials other than bamboo also, but bamboo works best.

Tips for Traveling by Raft

Always test your raft before committing to taking it across a water body.

Keep near the shore if possible and head to the bank if the raft gets out of control.

If rafting between islands, do it so the ebb takes you out and the high tide takes you to the new island. Study the currents by floating something you can observe.

If there are several rafts put one out in front as a scout. It should have the most capable members of the group and carry minimal equipment.

Use a pole to move the raft through shallow water. Use an oar through deep water.

Stay near the inside edge of river bends. The current will be slower.

Tie all equipment to the raft and make sure nothing trails over the edges.

Tie everyone to the raft (use a bowline around the waist), except in swift water. Lifelines should allow free movement but should not trail in the water.

Avoid obstructions.

When you come across rapids (or other dangerous ground) do the following:

- Unload the raft and secure it to the bank.
- Carry all equipment downstream by land.
- If the raft is too heavy to carry past the obstacle, place at least one member downstream of the raft. He/they should be at a safe spot where they will be able to recover it.
- Release the raft.
- Be sure to make repairs if needed.

At night secure the raft well and take shelter on high ground away from the river.

Swimming Across

Swimming across a river is a last resort move, but you may have to.

When swimming across a river you must allow for the drag of

the current. Choose your exit point and then choose an entry point upstream. How far upstream you need to enter depends on the strength of the current and how strong of a swimmer you are. Use your best judgment.

Use the aggressive swimming technique (freestyle with your head above water).

When there is more than one swimmer it is a good idea to pair (or triple if there is an odd number) them up. Pair a good swimmer that knows proper rescue techniques with a weak one so he can help if needed.

Improvised Flotation Aids

Any medium-sized object that floats can aid you when swimming across a body of water. A football, styrofoam cooler, floating log, etc.

Lashing together smaller empty containers also works well in slow water.

Tie your flotation device to your wrist and grab onto it if you get tired. You could also hug it with one arm although you would need to improvise your stroke. Sidestroke would work well for this.

Floating Pack

Waterproofing your pack as described before will give it some buoyancy.

If you know you will need the pack as a floatation device, trap air inside the pack liner before sealing it off.

It is also a good idea to then put your whole bag inside one larger waterproof bag. This gives an extra layer of waterproofing and means you can trap more air before entering the water. This outer layer will also prevent the actual pack from becoming waterlogged.

Tether your pack to your wrist using a quick release knot so it is easy to detach it if needed. Also, it is best if the tether is long.

You can hold onto your pack as you swim to use it for buoyancy. Another way is to push it in front of you while using the aggressive stroke. If the pack gets waterlogged, let it go so you can swim and then pull it to shore by the tether.

Bogs, Swamps, Quicksand, etc

Besides rivers, lakes, and the ocean, there are other types of water bodies that you may come across. These include bogs, swamps, quicksand, quagmires, and more.

Do not try to walk across them. Lifting your feet while standing will make you sink further.

Go around them or build an improvised bridge using logs, branches, or whatever is around. If this is not viable, there are other specific methods you can use.

Bogs and Swamps

You can cross a bog or swamp by lying face down with your arms and legs spread. Use a flotation device and slowly swim/pull yourself along. Keep your body horizontal.

Quicksand

Quicksand is a mixture of sand and water that sucks down objects that put weight on its surface. It usually occurs on flat shores, in silt-choked rivers with shifting watercourses, and near the mouths of large rivers. You can test for quicksand by throwing a small stone into the suspected area. It will sink in quicksand.

Although it has more suction, it is possible to cross quicksand in the same manner as bogs and swamps.

The following information is from Sam Fury's Disaster Survival Handbook.

www.SurvivalFitnessPlan.com/Disaster-Survival-Handbook

Start of Extract

When walking in quicksand country carry a pole as it will help you get out.

If You Fall In

Remain calm and use slow movements. Lay the pole on the surface of the quicksand. Use it to guide you onto your back in a floating position, with your arms and legs spread out.

Shift the pole under your hips at right angles to your spine.

Pull out your legs, one after the other, and move to the nearest solid ground.

End of Extract

Dense Vegetation

When swimming in dense vegetation stay near the surface. Thrashing about will get you in trouble. Use a gentle breaststroke and peel away the vegetation around you as you pass through.

Mangrove Swamps

Mangrove swamps are usually found along tropical coastlines. They are best crossed during low tide.

If you are inland trying to get to the ocean you can work your way through a narrow grove of trees.

When you are trying to get inland you are better off going to the small watercourses (streams or channels).

Always be on the lookout for crocodiles. If you see one, leave the water and get over the mangrove roots.

If the amount of water in the swamp allows it, build a raft.

Back Bays

Back bays are muddy islands found behind the dunes near the ocean. They are very tiring to cross. If you must, it is better to find the deep water sections so you can swim as opposed to trekking through the soft mud. Failing that, look for firmer bottom terrain such as sand, shell or stone. Trying to cross over the muddy islands is a bad idea as they are usually too soft.

SELF-RESCUE BOWLINE

The self-rescue bowline is good to learn in case you find yourself in a "man-overboard" situation or something similar. It is tying a bowline around your waist with only one hand.

Wrap the rope around your waist so that both the standing and running ends are to your front with your body (waist) between them. In this demonstration the running end is on your right.

Hold the running end in your right hand allowing at least 15cm of rope beyond your hand.

Without letting go of the running end bring it over the standing part to make a crossing point.

Bring it up though the gap created between your body and the crossing point. The rope will be wrapped around your hand.

Using your fingers, but without letting go of the rope, pass the running end under the standing part just beyond the first crossing point. This creates a second crossing point.

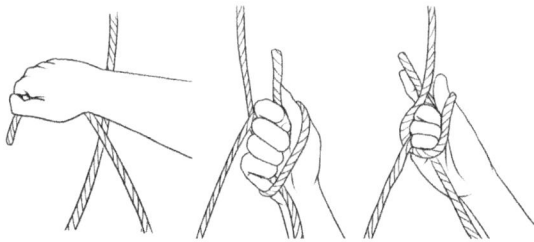

Continue to maneuver the running end with your fingers so that it feeds between the two crossing points. It feeds from the top down. It should end with you holding the running end.

Once that is accomplished pull your hand out from the loop on your wrist bringing the running end with you. Pull the knot tight.

INFLATING YOUR CLOTHES

Being stranded in the water and having to tread water to stay afloat expends precious energy. When you are wearing long clothes you can trap air inside them to help you float.

These methods work best with waterproof materials. For cotton clothing, keep the material that is out of the water wet to prevent air escaping.

Inflating Your Top

As you tread water (feet only), pull up your collar and bunch your shirt around your mouth to make a tight seal. Keep your nose out in the open.

Breathe in through your nose and exhale out your mouth into your shirt. Direct air into your shoulder area by leaning forward.

Inflating Your Trousers

If you cannot take your trousers off over your shoes, remove them. Tie the laces together, and then hang them around your neck.

Remove your pants, do the zip up, and tie the bottom of the trouser legs together.

Inflate your trouser legs using either the blow, sling, or splash method.

After inflating your pants keep the waistband underwater.

Put your head between the legs and hug the pants with the fly facing your body. Fold or twist the waistband closed to create a seal. You can rest your head back on the knot.

Keep the exposed material wet by splashing water on it.

When needed, open the waistband (while keeping it underwater) and scoop more air in.

Blow Method

This method is best for weak swimmers.

Hold the pants the right way up by the waistband, with the fly facing you. Take a deep breath and go underwater with the pants. Blow air into them.

Keeping the pants underwater, take another breath and blow more air into them. Repeat this until they filled with air.

Sling Method

Hold the trousers behind your head by the waistband ensuring you keep it open.

Using a forceful motion, sling the pants over your head in front of you and into the water to fill them with air.

Splash Method

Hold the waistband open underwater with one hand, fly facing up and trousers on the surface. Use your other hand inside the waistband to scoop water and air bubbles into your trousers. Scoop fast. The water will pass through leaving the air trapped.

COLD WATER SURVIVAL

Being immersed in cold water will sap your breath and energy quicker than normal. Panicking will make things worse. You must relax and get out. Concentrate on deep breathing to calm your mind and body.

If you cannot get on dry land you have to do whatever you can to keep your body heat until help arrives.

- Button or zip up your clothes and keep them on
- Don't use up energy swimming unless you have a dry place to swim to
- Get as much of yourself out of the water as possible
- Use the H.E.L.P. or Huddle position

Once you get out of the water it is important to remove all your wet clothing, dry yourself off, and get warm. Watch yourself and others for signs of hypothermia and treat as necessary.

More information about hypothermia and other cold-related illnesses is in the bonus section.

H.E.L.P

H.E.L.P. is an acronym for the Heat Escape Lessening Posture. It is the position to adopt when you are alone in the water and want to conserve your body heat.

The general idea of H.E.L.P. is to protect your major areas of heat loss, i.e., armpits, groin, head, neck, and rib cage.

When you are wearing a life-jacket, keep your head out of the water and lean back on it. Fold your arms and hug your jacket close to your body.

Cross your lower legs and bring your knees as high on your chest as you can.

If you do not have a life jacket, do your best to get as close to H.E.L.P. as possible.

Huddle Position

The huddle position is H.E.L.P. for groups of people (2+). Huddling together in a group has benefits such as:

- Lessen loss of body heat
- Increase morale

- Be easier to spot for rescuers
- Stronger swimmers can aid weaker ones

To adopt the huddle position, form a ring and group together. Everyone groups together as close as possible. Use your arms and legs to wrap around each other. Place those in need (such as children) in the middle.

Falling Through Ice

Escaping from a fall into ice water is not easy and the result can be deadly.

DO NOT PRACTICE THIS IN ICE WATER!

Go through the motions in a pool instead.

When you first fall into ice water you will start to hyperventilate. Try to stay calm and keep your head above the water. Taking deep breaths may help but do not breathe in the water.

After 1 to 3 minutes the shock response will begin to wear off. Now you have about 10 minutes to get out before you fall unconscious.

Once you have got your hyperventilation under control, find where you first fell in. You want to get out where you know it was strong enough to support your weight. Going to where you came from is your best bet.

Place your hands on the surface and pull yourself up while staying as horizontal as possible. Pulling yourself straight up will be far less effective and a waste of energy.

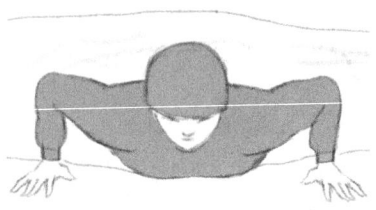

Kick your legs as your creep yourself out of the water. It will be very slippery.

Once you are out of the water, lie flat on the ice and roll away.

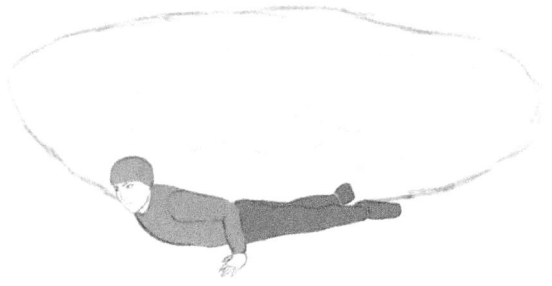

Rolling away keeps your weight distributed. It has less of a chance of creating further cracks in the ice.

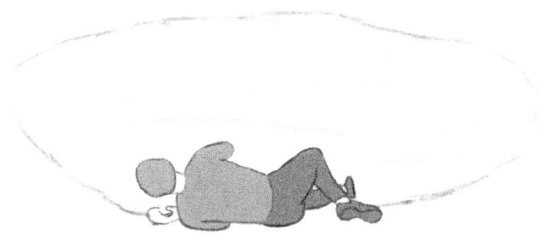

If you know you will be crossing ice country it is very wise to get some ice picks. They will make it far easier to pull yourself out of the water, although it will still be difficult.

If you cannot get out, then you need to conserve your heat and energy. Put your arms on the ice and keep them there so they freeze to the surface. This way, when you become unconscious you will have a better chance of not falling into the water.

Never go out to someone who has fallen into ice. Coach them on what to do from a safe distance and reach something out for them to hold onto such as a stick or rope.

Once out of the water get out of the wet clothes and get warm as soon as possible.

FLOOD

Avoiding Floods

Stay on higher ground, especially during and after sudden heavy rainfall when flash floods may occur.

Be extra careful after hurricanes, tidal waves and other natural disasters.

If in a Building

Stay in the building.

Prepare your survival kits and a raft.

Turn off gas, electricity and water at the mains.

Move to an upper floor or roof with a shelter.

If it is a sloping roof tie everyone on.

Unless forced to evacuate, stay put.

Note: If you live on the coast, evacuate.

Evacuating

Seek shelter on the highest ground possible.

Do not attempt to cross water unless certain that the water won't be higher than center of your vehicles wheels, or your knees if on foot.

If your car dies, abandon it.

Beware

- Bridges underwater may already have sections that have been swept away.
- Even a small drop in a hill can make a big difference in water level.

After the Flood

Contamination (of food, water etc.) is high.

Burn the dead.

Do not eat fresh food that has come in contact with flood water.

Don't risk eating animal corpses.

Do not walk around in, drink or bathe in flood water.

If cans of food have been exposed to the water wash them off with soap and clean, hot water before opening them.

Purify all water.

SURVIVAL AT SEA

Abandoning Ship

When you suspect you may need to abandon ship, or if your plane is going to crash in the ocean, put on warm (preferably woolen) clothing.

Cover as much of your body as you can and put on a life jacket.

Gather whatever survival provisions you can and get to a life boat.

Do not exceed the maximum passengers in a life vessel. Have the healthy hang off the side and swap regularly.

If You Have to Jump

- Throw something that floats in first and jump to it.
- Wait until you are off the ship before inflating your life-jacket.
- Once in the sea, get upwind and away from the sinking vessel.

If in the Water Without a Floatation Device

Attract the attention of a life-raft using noise and light.

Grab whatever you can that you could use to build a raft.

If there is a chance of underwater explosion swim on your back.

Keep composed and swim steadily upwind of the sinking vessel.

Swim under any danger, e.g., fire.

How to Improvise a Flotation Device with a Pair of Trousers

Knot the bottoms of the legs.

Hold the trousers behind your head by the waistband.

Sharply bring them over your head in front of you to fill them with air.

Hold the waist below water to trap the air.

If you need more air, go underwater and breathe into the pants.

If in Cold Water

Button or zip up your clothes and keep them on.

Don't use up energy swimming unless you have a dry place to swim to.

Get as much of yourself out of the water as possible.

Hold your knees to your chest to reduce core heat loss.

If There is a Group of You

- Face each other in a tight circle, holding onto each other.

Once Out of the Cold Water

Remove wet clothing.

Get dry and warm.

If in a Life-Raft

Wait until you are clear of the wreck before inflating it unless you can board it and stay dry.

Inflate the life-raft so it is firm, but not too hard. Compensate for the surrounding temperature (heat makes air expand).

Do not jump into it.

Check for leaks and inflation level at least once daily.

If you see little bubbles it is a sign of leaks. They must be repaired ASAP.

Make sure nothing can puncture it and waterproof everything that requires it.

Secure all passengers and equipment to it.

To Board a Life-Raft From the Water

- Move to one end (not the side).
- Put one leg over the edge and roll inside.

If the Life-Raft has a Line Attached

- Grab the line from the opposite side of where it is attached.
- Brace your feet against the life-raft and pull yourself in.
- Expect the other end of the life-raft to come up.
- This method can be improvised to right an overturned life-raft.

To Help Someone Else on Board

- Hold them by their shoulders.
- Have them lift one leg over the end of the raft (if possible).
- Roll them in.

Survival at Sea

If rescue is likely and there is no land in sight, or you are near regular shipping lanes, wait close to the crash site for rescue for at least 72 hours.

If you see land or know that it is near head for it.

Assign lookouts on short shifts. Look out for signs of life, land, rescue, leaks and anything that could be useful.

Keep your position by making a sea anchor. Tie weighted objects to a line.

Ration water and food immediately, even if you expect rescue.

Use whistles and lights to maintain contact with others if visibility is poor.

Movement at Sea

Using the Current

- Deflate the raft a little so it rides low in the water.
- Deploy your sea anchor.
- Keep low in the raft.

Using the Wind

- If you improvise a sail prevent capsize by holding the

bottom of it with your hands so that you can quickly release it if there is sudden gust of wind.
- Inflate the raft so it rides higher.
- Pull in your sea anchor.
- Sit up so your body catches the wind.

In Rough Waters

- Keep low.
- Stream the sea anchor from the bow (front).
- Tying life vessels together will improve stability.

Signs of Land

A constant wind with a decreasing swell. Land is wind-ward.

A green tint on the underside of clouds.

Isolated cumulus clouds.

Muddy water indicates silt from a large river mouth.

Lighter colored water indicates shallow water.

Seabirds fly away from land before noon and return to it in the afternoon.

Odors and sounds of land including smoke, vegetation, surf, animals etc.

Cumulus clouds are "puffy" with flat bases.

Choosing a Landing Point

Wait until daylight.

It is preferable to land on the downwind side of islands.

Select a point where it will be easy to beach or swim ashore

Approaching the Shore

Note the landscape (high ground, vegetation, water courses etc.).

Choose a meeting point in case you get separated.

Secure all your gear to your body and have a floatation aid ready.

Stay in the raft for as long as possible.

Take down the sail.

Put a sea anchor out to keep you pointing at the shore unless you are going through coral.

Head for gaps in the surf. Waves usually occur in sets of seven, from small to large.

Steer clear of rocks and/or ice and other obstacles.

If possible, keep the sun out of your eyes.

Attempt to use the waves to carry you into shore.

Paddle hard.

In Heavy Surf

- Point towards the sea.
- Paddle into approaching waves.

To Avoid Getting Swept Back Out to Sea

- Make the life-raft as light as possible.
- Take out the sea anchor.

If the Under-Current is Taking you Back Out

- Partly fill the raft with water.
- Stream the anchor towards the shore.

If Swimming to Shore

Face the shore and sit with your feet about a meter below your head.

Take any impact on the bottoms of your feet.

If the Surf is High

- Swim towards the shore in the trough between waves.

If a Wave Going Out to Sea Approaches

- Go under it, then continue to the shore.

If You Get Caught in the Undertow

- Remain calm and swim to the surface.
- Lie as close to the surface as possible.
- Swim parallel to the shore-line until you find a better place to go to shore.

Dear Reader,

Thank you for reading **Survival Swimming.**

If you enjoyed it, please leave a review on Amazon. It helps more than most people think. You can do that here:

www.SurvivalFitnessPlan.com/Survival-Swimming-Review-Amazon

For any feedback on how to improve this or any of my books you can contact me here:

www.SurvivalFitnessPlan.com/Contact

You can claim your bonus freebies at:

www.SurvivalFitnessPlan.com/Book-Bonus-Freebies

Download the freebies for the Swim Workouts and Water Rescue Skills book.

The password is: SWPFS*$56

And you can get FREE training schedules and more by joining our newsletter:

www.SurvivalFitnessPlan.com/Free-Downloads

Thanks again for your support,

Sam Fury.

AUTHOR RECOMMENDATIONS

This is Your Ultimate Fitness Program

This is the last fitness manual you'll ever need, because it is functional training at it's best!

Get it now.

www.SurvivalFitnessPlan.com/Survival-Fitness

This is the Only Wilderness Medicine Book You Need

Discover what you need to heal yourself, because a little knowledge goes a long way!

Get it now.

www.SurvivalFitnessPlan.com/Wilderness-Travel-Medicine

SURVIVAL FITNESS PLAN TRAINING MANUALS

Health and Fitness

Keep your body in optimal condition with minimal effort. The health and fitness series covers:

- **Nutrition and conditioning.** The 2 fundamentals for health and fitness.
- **Yoga.** Making Yoga a part of you daily routine will keep your mind and body healthy and in sync. Certain Yoga sequences are also a good alternative cure for many ailments.
- **Massage Therapy.** For prevention and healing of training injuries as well as general relaxation.

www.SurvivalFitnessPlan.com/Health-Fitness-Series

Survival Fitness

When in danger you have two options. Fight or Flight.

This series contains training manuals on the best methods of flight. Together with self defense, you can train in them for general health and fitness.

- **Parkour.** All the parkour skills you need to overcome obstacles in your path.
- **Climbing.** Focusing on essential bouldering techniques.
- **Riding.** Essential mountain bike riding techniques. Go as fast as possible in the safest manner.

- **Swimming.** Swimming for endurance and/or speed using the most efficient strokes.

www.SurvivalFitnessPlan.com/Survival-Fitness-Series

Self Defense

The Self Defense Series has volumes on some of the martial arts used as a base in SFP Self Defense.

It also contains the SFP Self Defense training manuals. SFP Self Defense is an efficient and effective form of minimalist self defense.

www.SurvivalFitnessPlan.com/Self-Defense-Series

Escape Evasion, and Survival

SFP escape, evasion, and survival skills (EES) focus on minimalism. It is EES using little to no special equipment.

- **Escape and Evasion.** The ability to escape capture and hide from your enemy.
- **Urban and Wilderness Survival.** Being able to live off the land in all terrains.
- **Emergency Roping.** Basic climbing skills and improvised roping techniques.
- **Water Rescue.** Life-saving water skills based on surf life-saving and military training course competencies.
- **Wilderness First Aid.** Modern medicine for use in emergency situations.

Specific subjects covered include entry and exit techniques, evasive driving, hostile negotiation tactics, lock-picking, urban survival, wilderness survival, computer hacking, and more.

www.SurvivalFitnessPlan.com/Escape-Evasion-Survival-Series

ABOUT THE AUTHOR

Sam has had an interest in self-preservation & survival for as long as he can remember. This has lead to years of training and career-related experience in related subjects.

He describes himself as a "Survivalist, Minimalist, Traveler" and spends his time exploring the world, learning new skills, and sharing his knowledge through his books.

www.SurvivalFitnessPlan.com

- facebook.com/SurvivalFitnessPlan
- twitter.com/Survival_Fitnes
- pinterest.com/survivalfitnes
- goodreads.com/SamFury
- bookbub.com/authors/sam-fury
- amazon.com/author/samfury

Made in the USA
Middletown, DE
31 July 2019